Studying God's Word

Book D

Exploring the Truths

of the Life of Christ for

the Young Reader

Darrel A. Trulson

Published by
Christian Liberty Press
502 West Euclid Avenue
Arlington Heights, Illinois 60004

Printed in the United States of America

Dedicated to
Grandma Orne,

who through her good works
and faithfulness to the Lord Jesus,
has been an inspiration
to many.

Table of Contents

Page Number

Acknowledgments

When working on a project of this scope, there are inevitably many people to whom thanks are due. As the *Studying God's Word* series grows and matures, I am continually brought to terms with my own inadequacies, not only as a writer but as a person. Were it not for the love, support, and encouragement of my family and friends, these books would never be written. So to everyone who has not only stood with me, but also been an integral and necessary part of this project, I give you my deepest and warmest heart-felt thanks.

I especially want to thank Mike McHugh for his invaluable friendship, direction and guidance. These last two years have certainly had their share of trials and changes, but through it all the Lord has been faithful. Thank you for your continued trust and support in me.

Thanks to Dad and Mom for their love and encouragement. Thank you for being there when the waters were both calm and rough.

Thanks to my wife Debbie, and my five children – Derek, Daniel, Joshua, Michael, and Lauren – for their love, patience, and understanding. My love for you grows with each and every passing day. Thank you for being there by my side, helping me to maintain my perspective, and forgiving me when I fail.

Most of all, thanks to the Lord Jesus, through Whom everything is possible. God bless us all.

Preface

The primary goal of the *Studying God's Word* series is to encourage students to conform their thinking and actions to the standard of God's revealed Word. When students begin to bring every one of their thoughts into captivity to God's Word, they begin to realize the joy of being conformed to the image of Jesus Christ.

In this series, students are presented with Biblical doctrine and important principles to help them develop strong Christian character traits. Students are also provided with a wealth of personal examples from the lives of God's people that illustrate the truths they need to comprehend.

More than ever before, young people need to be equipped with the whole armor of God's Word so they can withstand the fiery darts of the wicked one. It is the firm belief of our publishing ministry that the Holy Scriptures are the only reliable foundation for faith and life.

May the Lord use this Bible study series to equip his children with the spiritual weapons that they need to fight the good fight of faith.

Michael J. McHugh
Curriculum Director

Dr. Paul D. Lindstrom
Superintendent of Schools

How to Use This Book

If you are like most people, you may neglect to read the instructions or directions for something until you are half finished with it, and then discover you did something wrong. In order to understand this book and learn the most from it, **please read this section first!**

Each lesson will contain a few paragraphs in which the author teaches some principles from the text and applications for the student to make in his life. This is followed by a few questions or an exercise covering the background reading. The last two pages of the lesson will be a puzzle or project which ties in with the overall theme of the lesson.

Every lesson will have a memory verse for the child to study and learn. The student is not required to memorize this verse, but it is strongly encouraged. All memory verses, lessons, and questions have been taken from the King James Version of the Bible unless otherwise noted.

It is important to emphasize that, if the student is unable to read the lessons or write the answers to the questions, the parent or teacher is to read and/or write the answers for the child. The author recognizes that children of various ages and abilities will be using this book. An attempt has been made to maintain a balance between challenging the child, while not making the book overly burdensome or "busy." It is with this hope that in the areas where this book is either too easy or too difficult, that the instructor will fill the void with his own love, patience, and attention to the needs of the student.

As you work through these lessons with your child, you will not only discover the joy there is in studying God's Word, but also the difficulty of answering questions which this book does not address or that you are not prepared to answer. As time permits, consult commentaries, Bible dictionaries, Bible encyclopedias, and other kinds of reference material at your disposal. The information gained from these sources will be invaluable to you as you address the difficult questions which may arise.

Regrettably, time and space do not allow us to cover the whole Bible in this book. The Old Testament for the young reader is covered in *Studying God's Word Book C*. The Old Testament in a chronological format is presented in *Studying God's Word Book E* and *Studying God's Word Book F*. The Gospels and the life of Christ are reviewed in *Studying God's Word Book G*. The book of Acts is taught in *Studying God's Word Book H*. The rest of the New Testament will be covered in subsequent volumes of this series.

The goal and purpose of this book comes directly from Joshua 1:8: "This book of the Law shall not depart out of thy mouth; but thou shalt meditate therein day and night, that thou mayest observe to do according to all that is written therein: for then thou shalt make thy way prosperous, and then thou shalt have good success." The sincere hope and prayer of the author is that God will use this book as a tool in the spiritual instruction and guidance of your child. May the Lord grant you wisdom and grace as you seek to raise your child in the truths and principles of His Word.

Remember, children need a steady and balanced dose of encouragement, discipline, and love. Do not expect young children to perform each and every exercise flawlessly. God is the only one who can perform each task perfectly. Your steady support and encouragement will permit your student to study in an atmosphere which will promote high standards of achievement.

Let us not forget that our greatest testimony is to our own children and family.

The Birth of the Savior
Matthew 1:18-25; Luke 2:1-20

Christmas is the season of year we celebrate the birth of the Lord Jesus Christ. It is a time of joy and excitement, because we are reminded that God gave man the greatest present of all -- the gift of His only begotten Son.

Even though as we read this, it may not be the Christmas season, it is good to keep the joy of the holiday all year long in our hearts. Apart from the month of December, how often do we truly think of the importance of God coming to the earth as a man. If Jesus had not been born, we would not have salvation from our sins. For when God became a man, He set into motion a series of events which eventually led to His death and resurrection. Through Christ's suffering and death He made the way for us to have eternal life in heaven; and to think it all started with a baby in a manger.

Take a few moments today to thank your Heavenly Father for giving us the gift of eternal life through His Son, the Lord Jesus Christ. Although it may not be Christmas, it is good to be reminded that we can have joy in our hearts, because Jesus was born in Bethlehem to be the perfect sacrifice for our sins.

> I am come that they might have life, and that they might have it more abundantly. John 10:10b

The Birth of the Savior

Read each question and fill in the blanks from the answers in the shaded box.

1. Mary was found with child of the _____. (Matthew 1:18)

2. The _____ of the Lord appeared to _____ in a dream. (Matthew 1:20)

3. Jesus would save His _____ from their _____. (Matthew 1:21)

4. In those days a _____ went out from Caesar that all the _____ should be _____. (Luke 2:1)

5. Mary wrapped the baby in _____ clothes and laid Him in a _____. (Luke 2:7)

6. Shepherds were keeping _____ over their _____ by _____. (Luke 2:8)

7. The glory of the _____ shone around the shepherds, and they were sore _____. (Luke 2:9)

8. The angel said, "Fear not, for I bring you _____ tidings of great _____. (Luke 2:10)

9. Glory to God in the _____, and on earth _____, good will toward men. (Luke 2:14)

10. Mary kept all these things, and _____ them in her _____. (Luke 2:19)

afraid	Holy Spirit	people
angel	Joseph	pondered
decree	joy	sins
flock	Lord	swaddling
good	manger	taxed
heart	night	watch
highest	peace	world

The Birth of the Savior

Read Matthew 1:18-25 and Luke 2:1-20 to complete the crossword puzzle.

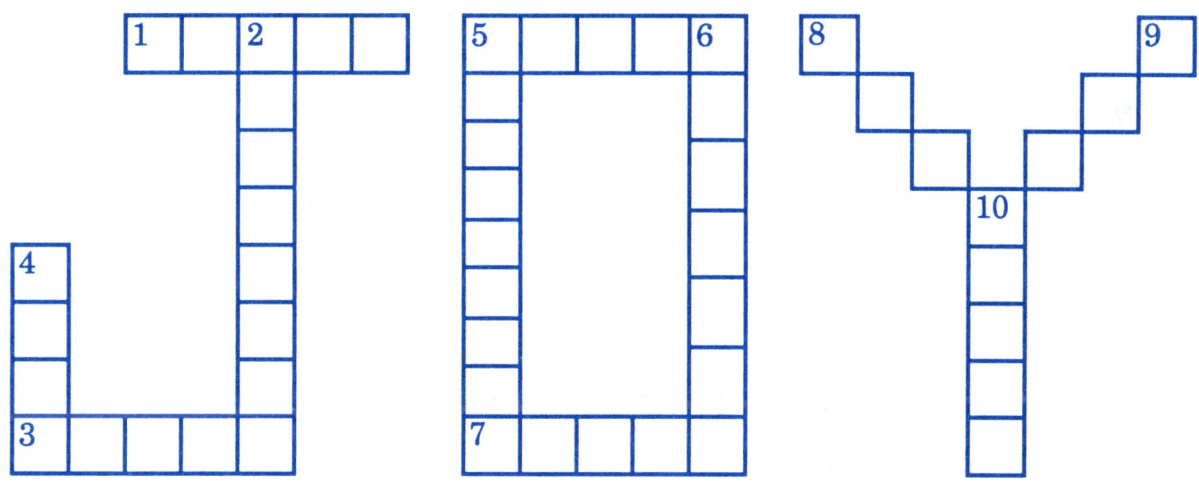

- Across -

1. Joseph was raised from this. (Matt. 1:24)
3. "Ye ____ find the babe wrapped in swaddling clothes." (Luke 2:12)
5. "Behold a virgin shall be with child, and shall bring ____ a Son." (Matt. 1:23)
7. When were the shepherds watching their flock? (Luke 2:8)

- Down -

2. Mary and Joseph's Son was to be called this. (Matt. 1:23)
4. "And it came to ____ in those days." (Luke 2:1)
5. "And she brought forth her ____ Son." (Luke 2:7)
6. "Glory to God in the ____." (Luke 2:14)
8. "And, lo, the angel of the ____ came upon them. (Luke 2:9)
9. What kind of tidings did the angel bring the shepherds? (Luke 2:10)
10. In whose city was a Savior born? (Luke 2:11)

Wise Men Still Seek Him
Matthew 2:1-12

A year or two after Christ was born in Bethlehem, several wise men came to visit Him. We do not know much about these individuals, only that they came from the east, and that they brought valuable gifts to give to the child king.

It is important to understand that men are only wise when they seek after God. The Apostle Paul wrote in I Corinthians chapter one, that what the non-Christian world considers wise is actually foolishness to God, and what is wise to God is foolishness to the world. This is because non-Christians do not place their priorities upon the Lord Jesus Christ. They would rather seek after their own selfish interests rather than follow the teachings of the Bible.

In order for us to be wise, we need to obey the Bible and believe in the Lord Jesus Christ as our personal Savior. True wisdom only comes from God. Proverbs 3:7 says, "Do not be wise in your own eyes; fear the Lord and turn away from evil." Like the wise men in this lesson who traveled many miles to visit Jesus, we will only be wise when we come to the Lord.

> But by His doing you are in Christ Jesus, who became to us wisdom from God, and righteousness, and sanctification, and redemption. I Corinthians 1:30 NASV

Wise Men Still Seek Him

Multiple choice -- circle the correct answer for each question.

1. Where was Jesus born? (Matthew 2:1)
    *Egypt
    *Bethlehem
    *Jerusalem
    *Nazareth

2. The wise men were looking for whom? (Matthew 2:2)
    *The King of the Jews
    *The chief priest
    *King Herod
    *Other wise men

3. What had the wise men seen in the east? (Matthew 2:2)
    *The sea
    *The sun
    *A desert
    *A star

4. When the King heard about the wise men, how did he feel? (Matthew 2:3)
    *He was happy
    *He was troubled
    *He was excited
    *He did not care

5. What did the King demand of the chief priests and scribes? (Matthew 2:4)
    *From where the wise men had come
    *Where the wise men were going
    *Where Christ should be born
    *Where to worship the young child

6. What did King Herod enquire of the wise men? (Matthew 2:7)
    *If he could one day become a wise man
    *From where they had come
    *The time the star appeared
    *If they had traveled far

7. What did Herod tell the wise men to do once they had found the young child? (Matthew 2:8)
   *Go back to the east
   *Bring word to him that he may worship the child
   *Make the young child a wise man
   *Tell the chief priests about this discovery

8. What stood over the young child? (Matthew 2:9)
   *The star
   *King Herod
   *The wise men
   *Mary and Joseph

9. How did the wise men feel when they saw the star? (Matthew 2:10)
   *Tired
   *They rejoiced with great joy
   *Sad
   *Ready to go back to Herod

10. What gifts did the wise men bring the child? (Matthew 2:11)
    *Gold, silver and precious stones
    *Myrrh, Frankincense and silver
    *Gold, Frankincense and precious stones
    *Frankincense, Gold and Myrrh

Wise Men Still Seek Him

Each of us have special gifts and abilities which we can bring to the Christ Jesus. Turn to page 123 and cut out the names of the gifts which you can give to the Lord. These words are different things which you can do to serve God. Pick the ones which are the most important to you and paste them onto the presents pictured below.

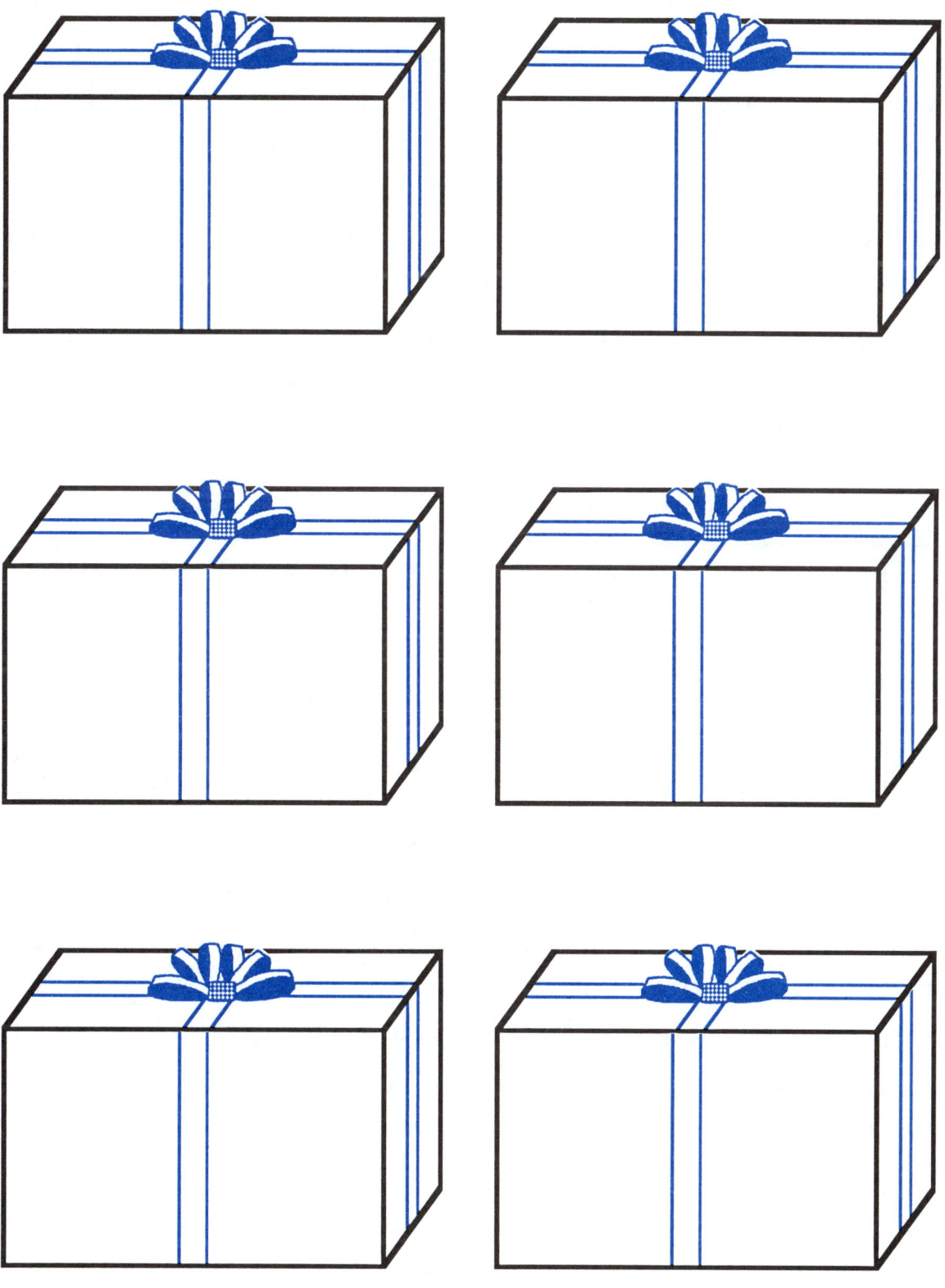

Lesson #3

Doing our Father's Business
Luke 2:41-52

Think for a moment about the different tasks and jobs you have to do around your home. Perhaps your parents ask you to wash the dishes or take out the garbage. Maybe you have a small garden where you grow vegetables or a few pets which you take for walks and feed. No doubt Jesus helped his earthly parents with the chores around their house. He may have helped his mother clean up their home, or maybe he worked with his dad as a carpenter. You see, even Jesus had things which he needed to do; however, most importantly, Jesus served His heavenly Father.

What are the things which you do for the Lord? Perhaps you go to church, read your Bible, pray and put some money in the offering. These are all important things to do because they show that we are serving God. When we love the Lord with our whole heart, we want to obey Him and do the things which make Him happy. This is what it means to "do our Father's business." By loving the Lord and doing what He commands, we show that we are His children.

As a young child, Jesus surprised the religious leaders in Jerusalem with his understanding of the Old

Testament Scriptures and the principles of God's Word. Those teachers were amazed because they did not expect that such great understanding could come from a young child. Even though Jesus was God, he still had to grow and learn like you and I. Christ went about His Father's business by studying the Scriptures and talking to the teachers in the temple. We too can go about our Father's business by reading the Bible and applying its truths to our lives.

> Let no man despise thy youth; but be thou an example of the believers, in word, in conversation, in charity, in spirit, in faith, in purity. I Timothy 4:12

Read each question and fill in the blanks with the correct answer.

1. When did Christ's parents go to Jerusalem? (Luke 2:41) _____

   _____

2. How old was Jesus when He went with His parents to Jerusalem? (Luke 2:42) _____

3. Where did Jesus tarry? (Luke 2:43) _____

4. Mary and Joseph supposed Jesus was where? (Luke 2:44) _____

   _____

5. Among whom did Mary and Joseph seek for Jesus? (Luke 2:44)

   _____

6. Where did they find Jesus? (Luke 2:46) _____

7. Mary and Joseph found Jesus sitting in the midst of whom? (Luke 2:46) _____

8. At what were the people who heard Jesus astonished? (Luke 2:47) _____

9. What did Jesus say he must be about? (Luke 2:49) _____

   _____

10. In what did Jesus increase? (Luke 2:52) _____

    _____

    _____

> At his understanding and answers
> Every year at the feast of the passover
> In Jerusalem
> In the temple
> In wisdom and stature, and in favour with God and man
> My Father's business
> The doctors
> Their kinsfolk and acquaintance
> To have been in the company
> Twelve years old

Doing our Father's Business

Find and circle the words listed in the word search puzzle. Words may be forward, backward, horizontal, vertical or diagonal.

```
A S T O N I S H E D T K
J O Q P A S S O V E R I
O R J T Z S U F L E M N
U R H E A R T E E I O S
R O T M R B S A W O T F
N W H P E U Z S T J H O
E I R L T S S T E U E L
Y N E E H I N A R I R K
A G E W S N E M L O W E
S S U B J E C T S E A E
J T I W I S D O M P M U
S N Q U E S T I O N S T
```

ASTONISHED	KINSFOLK	STATURE
BUSINESS	MOTHER	SUBJECT
FEAST	NAZARETH	TEMPLE
HEART	PASSOVER	THREE
JERUSALEM	QUESTIONS	TWELVE
JOURNEY	SORROWING	WISDOM

Christ's Baptism

Matthew 3:13-17; Mark 1:9-11; Luke 3:21-22

A favorite question of my children to ask whenever we talk about the life of our Lord is, "How can Jesus be God, if God is in heaven?" This is a hard question because it deals with an idea called the "Trinity". The "trinity" teaches that there is one God in three persons; God the Father, God the Son, and God the Holy Spirit.

At Christ's baptism, we have a wonderful illustration as to how the Trinity works. God the Son is baptized by John in the Jordan River; God the Holy Spirit descends upon him as a dove; and God the Father says, "This 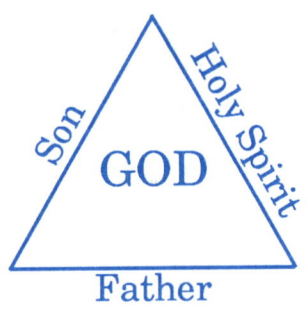 is my beloved Son, in whom I am well pleased." All three members of the Trinity had a role in this special event.

As you study the Bible you will continue to learn more about the "Trinity", and the roles of each member of the God-head. If you have difficulty remembering what the Trinity is, just think "Three in One." Three members -- one God.

> For there is one God, and one mediator between God and men, the man Christ Jesus. I Timothy 2:5

Christ's Baptism

Match the correct answer with the proper question.

1. _____ From where did Jesus come? (Matt. 3:13)

2. _____ By whom did John say he needed to be baptized? (Matt. 3:14)

3. _____ What did Jesus want to fulfill by being baptized? (Matt. 3:15)

4. _____ Where did Jesus go after he was baptized? (Matt. 3:16)

5. _____ Where was Jesus baptized by John? (Mark 1:9)

6. _____ How did the Spirit descend upon Christ? (Mark 1:10)

7. _____ What did Jesus see the heavens do? (Mark 1:10)

8. _____ Who descended upon Christ? (Luke 3:22)

9. _____ From where did a voice come? (Luke 3:22)

10. ___ Who did the voice say was Christ? (Luke 3:22)

a. Out of the water

b. Jesus

c. The Holy Ghost

d. In the Jordan

e. Open

f. Heaven

g. His beloved Son

h. Galilee

i. Like a dove

j. All righteousness

Color the pictures which show people doing good things. The pictures which show people doing bad things you are to leave blank.

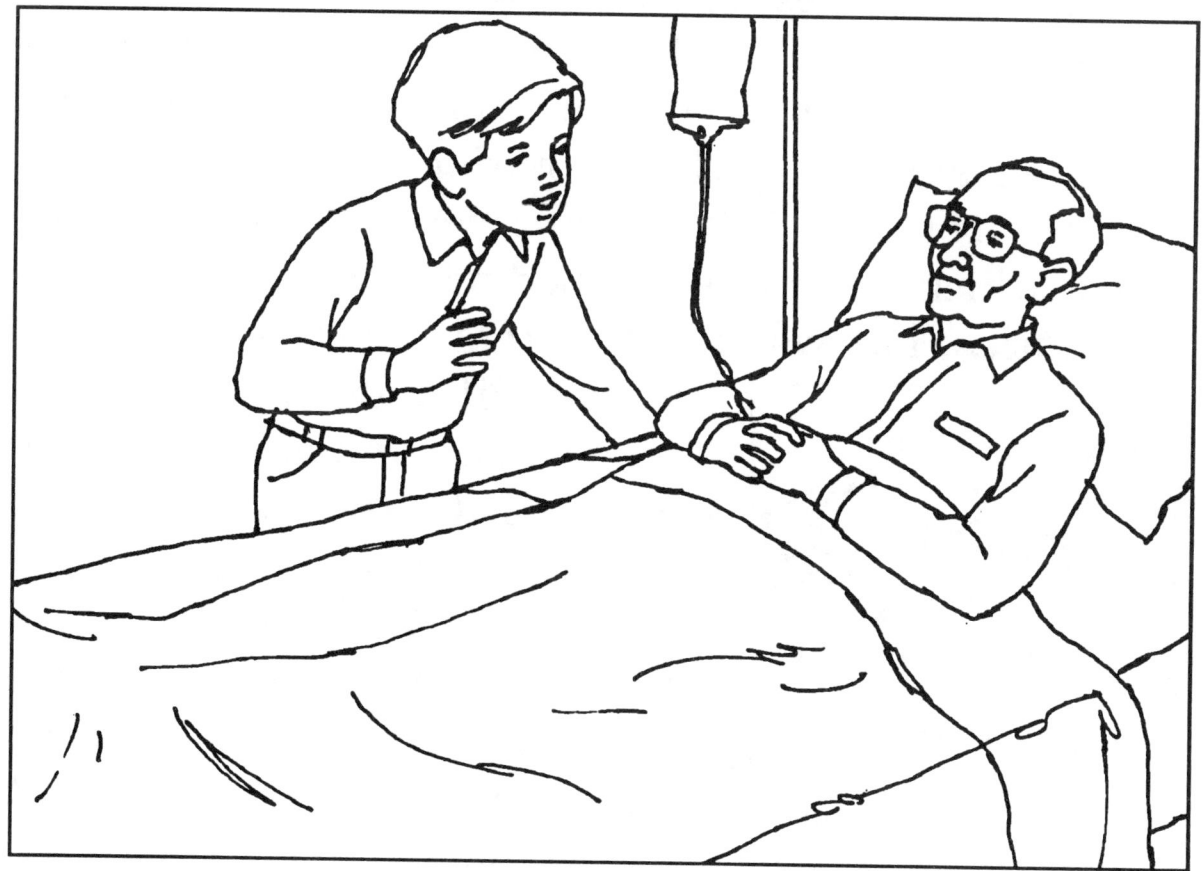

Christ's Temptation
Matthew 4:1-11; Mark 1:12-13; Luke 4:1-13

It is very hard to be good. No matter how we try or what we do, we always find ourselves getting into trouble. Even the great Apostle Paul said that the good things which he wanted to do he could not, because sin dwelled in him (Romans 7:14-25).

The reason we cannot be good is because we have sin in our hearts. It is only when the Lord Jesus saves us from our sin, that we are able to do the things which God considers to be good. Even after we are saved we still sin and need to ask the Lord to forgive us.

We may sometimes wonder -- how can God understand our struggle to be good, He never sinned? It is true that Christ never sinned, but the Bible teaches that our Lord suffered with temptation the same way we do. Hebrews 4:15 says, "For we have not an high priest which cannot be touched with the feeling of our infirmities; but was in all points tempted like as we are, yet without sin." It is not wrong to be tempted, only when we give into that temptation does it become sin. We can take hope in this fact that Jesus can understand the temptations we feel and the struggles we go through, because He also went through them.

There hath no temptation taken you but such as is common to man: but God is faithful, who will not suffer you to be tempted above that ye are able. I Corinthians 10:13a

Each of the pictures below has something to do with the temptation of Christ. Match up the correct Scripture reference with each picture. All passages are taken from Luke 4:1-13.

4:3   4:4   4:5

4:9   4:10   4:11

In the following story, a child is faced with a temptation. Read the story, and discuss the possible solutions with your parents or teacher. On the blank spaces at the end of the story, write the way you think it should end.

Tammy walked alongside of her mother as she pushed the cart down the aisle. They had been shopping all morning and she was excited because they had just picked out a new dress to wear to her birthday party on Saturday.

Just then, she saw something shiny out of the corner of her eye. "Oh Mother," Tammy exclaimed, "Wouldn't these barretts look nice with my new dress!"

"Yes they would Tammy," her mother said, glancing down at her watch, "But you will have to wait till later to get them. I only have enough money right now to pay for the dress."

Tammy was very disappointed, and the turned down corners of her mouth showed it. She liked her dress, but the barretts were just the things she needed to make the outfit look perfect.

Tammy stopped walking and watched her mother move ahead into the next department. Looking all around her to see if anyone was near by, she pushed her cart next to the barretts and gently pulled the set she wanted off the rack. She held the barretts against her head and gazed at them in the mirror; the pink and white bows on them were so dressy. Tammy thought that they made her appear much older and more mature.

"Well, my mother did not say that I couldn't get them." Tammy thought to herself. She just said she did not have the money to get them right now.

At first Tammy was satisfied to just wait, but then she remembered that the party was tomorrow and with all the other preparations, there would be no time to come back to the store for the barretts. Tammy sighed an aggravated little sigh and put the barretts back on the rack. As she looked up to see where her mother had gone she noticed that the saleslady was busy helping another customer and wasn't paying any attention to her.

It was just a tiny spark of an idea, but it took hold in Tammy's mind very quickly. Perhaps she could quietly slip that small package of barretts into her pocket and just walk out of the store with her mother. After all, she had money in her bank at home so she could tell her mother she bought them herself. The more Tammy thought about this the easier it seemed. Yet, just as quickly as this thought came into her mind, so also did the realization that this would be stealing. She wrestled with her choices briefly and then made her decision. . .

_____

_____

_____

_____

_____

_____

_____

_____

Born Again
John 3:1-36

What does it mean to be a Christian? Is a Christian someone who goes to church and reads his Bible? Yes, but a Christian is much more than that. A Christian is a person who believes that Christ died on the cross to take away his sins, and who has asked Jesus to live in his heart.

When we believe in the Lord Jesus a change takes place in our lives. We are "born again." This means that our sinful soul is washed clean, and the Holy Spirit dwells within us. Our soul, which was dead in sin, is now alive by faith in the Savior, Jesus Christ.

People may not outwardly see the change which takes place in our lives right away, but if they could look at our spiritual hearts, they could see the Holy Spirit guiding our actions and helping us to be good. As Christians, it is important that we live good lives and obey what the Bible teaches, but it is most important that we are "born again" by believing in the Lord Jesus as our personal Savior.

> For God so loved the world, that He gave His only begotten Son, that whosoever believeth in Him should not perish, but have everlasting life. John 3:16

Born Again

Read each question and fill in the blanks from the answers in the shaded box.

1. Except that a man be _____, he cannot see the _____. (John 3:3)

2. That which is born of the spirit is _____. (John 3:6)

3. If I have told you _____ things, and you believed not, how shall you believe, if I tell you of _____ things. (John 3:12)

4. As _____ lifted up the _____ in the wilderness, even so must the _____ be lifted up. (John 3:14)

5. God sent not his son into the _____ to _____ the world. (John 3:17)

6. He that _____ on Him is not _____. (John 3:18)

7. Men loved darkness rather than _____, because their deeds were _____. (John 3:19)

8. He that doeth _____ cometh to the light. (John 3:21)

9. A man can receive _____, except it be given him from heaven. (John 3:27)

10. The Father loveth the _____. (John 3:35)
    He that believeth on the Son hath everlasting _____. (John 3:36)

Believeth	Light
Born Again	Moses
Condemn	Nothing
Condemned	Serpent
Earthly	Son
Evil	Son of Man
Heavenly	Spirit
Kingdom of God	Truth
Life	World

Color the picture of Christ as He conquered sin and secured the way for His children to have everlasting life.

Born Again

Nicodemus came at night to talk to Christ Jesus. Help Nicodemus find his way through the maze to the Lord.

The Missing Piece
John 4:1-42

Within every person there is a spiritual emptiness which has to be filled with something. Some people fill this void with money, friends, and even false religions. The trouble is, people will never be truly happy or satisfied unless this emptiness is filled with the Lord Jesus Christ.

Have you ever put together a puzzle, only to find at the end that one piece was missing or the piece you had was the wrong one and did not fit. People are the same way, only the missing puzzle piece happens to be Christ Jesus. If we try to put anything else into the spiritual puzzle space in our lives, it just will not fit correctly. Our lives will never be truly complete until we purpose to love and serve God.

When Jesus spoke to the women at the well, like everyone else, He knew she was trying to fill her life with things besides God. He also knew she would never be happy or satisfied until she trusted in the Lord as her Savior.

The spiritual thirst which people experience is because their lives are empty. They have not committed their hearts to God and experienced the fullness which

Christ Jesus brings to a person's life. The Apostle Paul says it best when he writes in Ephesians 3:19, "And to know the love of Christ which passeth knowledge, that ye might be filled with all the fullness of God."

> If any man thirst, let him come unto me, and drink. John 7:37b

Fill in the missing letter in each circle from the story of the woman at the well. All passages are taken from John 4:1-42.

When Jesus was sitting by the ◯ell, a woman of Samaria came to draw water. Jesus said to her, "Give Me a ◯rink." (4:7)

The woman asked why since He was a ◯ew, that He would ask for a drink from a ◯amaritan ◯oman. For Jews had no dealings with Samaritans. (4:9)

Jesus said to the women that ◯veryone who drinks from this water will ◯hirst again; but whoever drinks of the ◯ater that I shall give him shall never thirst. And this water which I shall give him will be like a well ◯pringing up into ◯verlasting life. (4:14)

The woman said to ◯esus, "Sir give me this water, that I thirst not, neither come hither to draw." (4:15)

The ◯our cometh when ye shall neither in this mountain, nor yet at Jerusalem worship the ◯ather. But the hour cometh, and now is, when the true worshippers shall worship the Father in ◯pirit and in ◯ruth: for the Father seeketh such to worship him. God is spirit: and they that worship Him must worship Him in spirit and in truth. (4:21-24)

Jesus said to His ◯isciples, "My ◯eat is to do the will of Him that sent me, and to finish His ◯ork." (4:34)

Complete the vertical crossword by finding the missing words from the passage of Scripture and filling them in the blank squares. There is a secret message in the middle boxes, can you find it?

John 4:7-19
There cometh a [6] of Samaria to draw water: Jesus saith unto her, Give me to drink. (For his [8] were gone away unto the [19] to buy meat.) Then saith the woman of Samaria unto Him, How is it that thou, being a Jew, askest [9] of me, which am a woman of Samaria? For the [1] have no [7] with the [2]. [18] answered and said unto her, Whosoever drinketh of this water shall thirst [13]: but whosoever drinketh of the water that I shall give him shall never thirst; but the [3] that I shall give him shall be in him a well of water [16] up into everlasting [10]. The woman saith unto Him, [17], give me this water, that I [4] not, neither come hither to draw. Jesus saith unto her, Go, call thy husband, and come [15]. The woman answered and said, I have no husband. Jesus said unto her, Thou hast well said, I have no [5]: for thou has had [12] husbands; and he whom thou now hast is not thy husband: in that saidst thou truly. The woman saith unto Him, Sir, I [14] that thou art a [11].

The Missing Piece

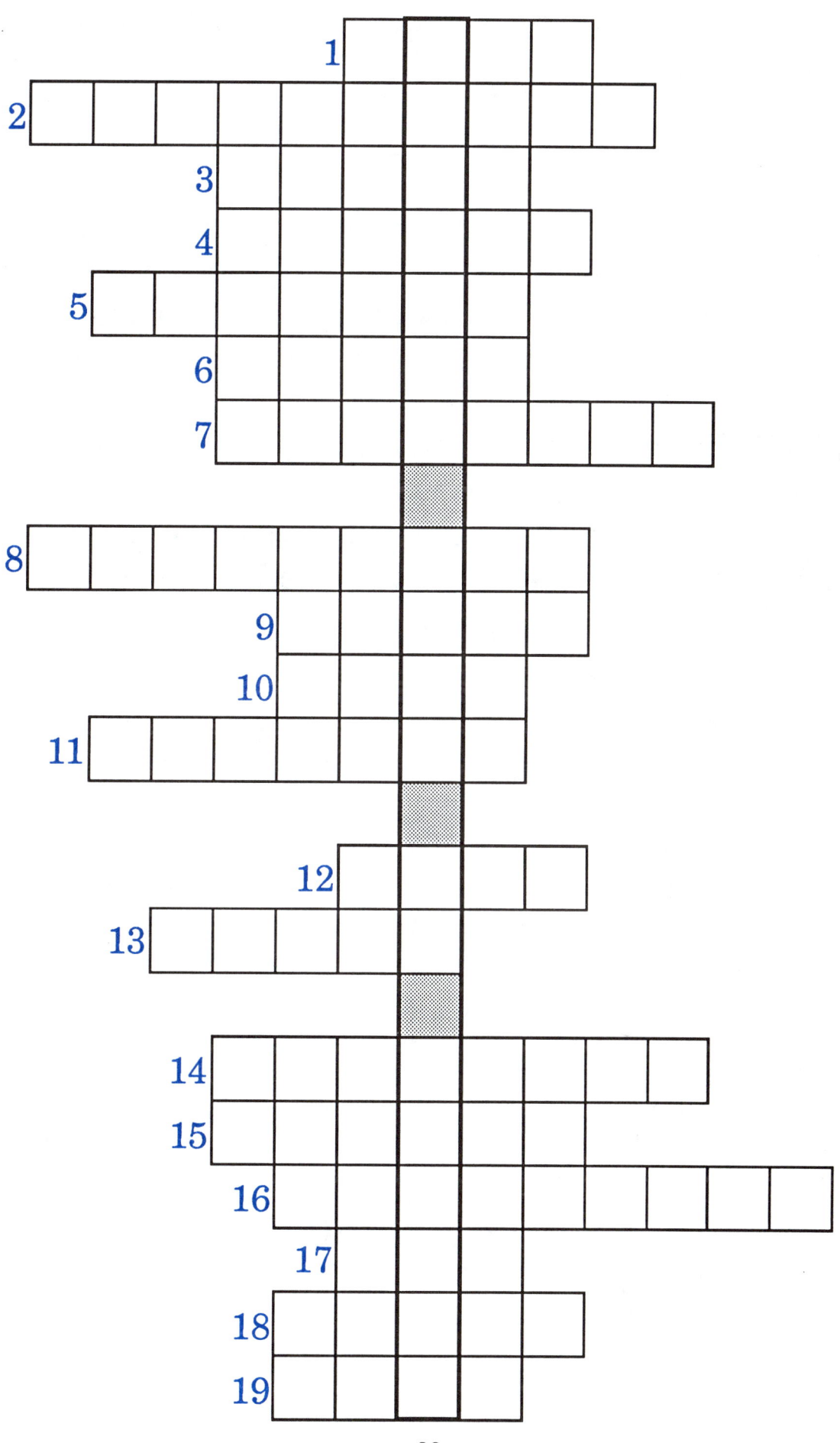

Healing by the Pool
John 5:1-47

Most children like to go swimming, especially if the weather is hot and the water is cool. Back in the Bible times there was a pool where sick people could get better if they jumped into it at the right moment.

One day Jesus met a man by this pool. The man could not get into the water because he was unable to walk. No one took the time to help this person so he could be healed. This man was handicapped because he was not able to do the things which we do every day and often take for granted.

Do you know anyone who has a disability? Maybe even you have a handicap. People can have many different kinds of disabilities. Some people may not be able to walk; whereas, others are unable to see or hear. There are many reasons why a person may be handicapped. However, we need to take the time to help and be especially considerate toward them.

We do not have the power to heal like Christ did; however, we do have the power to help people with their disabilities. Let us purpose to use the abilities the Lord has given us to be kind and gracious to everyone around us. If we will be faithful in this matter, God will surely bless us.

Healing by the Pool

And whosoever shall give to drink unto one of these little ones a cup of cold water only in the name of a disciple, verily I say unto you, he shall in no wise lose his reward. Matthew 10:42

Read each question and write the answer from the text for this lesson.

1. How many porches did the pool in Bethesda have? (John 5:2)

   _____

2. How many years did the man have an infirmity? (John 5:5)

   _____

3. On what day was the man cured? (John 5:10) _____

4. Why did the Jews persecute and try to slay Jesus? (John 5:16)

   _____

5. Why did the Jews want to kill Christ even more? (John 5:18) ____

   _____

   _____

6. What did the Father commit unto the Son? (John 5:22) _____

   _____

7. How should men honor the Son? (John 5:23) _____

   _____

8. Who has everlasting life? (John 5:24) _____

   _____

   _____

   _____

9. What did the people not have in them? (John 5:42) _____

   _____

10. Who wrote of Christ? (John 5:46) _____

   _____

Write the missing words in the correct location. You will have to use your Bible and look up Colossians 3:12-14 to find the answers. These verses explain how Christians are to behave. If you do not have a King James Version Bible, ask your teacher to help you with a different translation.

Put on therefore, as the elect of God, _____ and _____, bowels of _____, _____, _____ of mind, _____, _____; _____ one another and _____ one another, if any man have a quarrel against any: even as Christ forgave you, so also do ye. And above all these things put on _____, which is the bond of _____.

Healing by the Pool

Decode the symbols to understand the secret message. The key is in the box at the side of this page.

Fishers of Men
Matthew 4:17-25; Mark 1:14-20

When Jesus told his disciples that He wanted them to be fishers of men, He was saying that He wanted them to go out and bring people into His Kingdom.

If you have ever been fishing, you will know that the fish do not just jump into your boat when you row across the lake. One needs to put good bait on the hook, cast out the line, and try to find a place where there are some fish. As Christians, we need to also bait our hook with the gospel, preach and teach it with our lives and find a place where there will be people who will watch and listen to our message.

We are each commanded by the Lord to take an active part in His Kingdom by becoming fishers of men. By casting out our line, we are sharing the good news of Christ's resurrection and eternal life with those who are around us. When we go fishing we do not always catch fish, and when we witness about the Lord, not everyone will become Christians; however, unless we are talking about Jesus, who will ever hear what we have to say? Romans 10:14 says, how can the unsaved hear, unless there is a preacher. We cannot expect to catch fish unless we put our hook into the water. We are God's fishermen to the world.

Fishers of Men

Let your light so shine before men, that they may see your good works, and glorify your Father which is in heaven. Matthew 5:16

Multiple choice -- circle the correct answer for each question.

1. What were Peter and Andrew doing when Jesus called them?
    (Matthew 4:18)
     *Talking to each other
     *Sleeping
     *Casting a net into the sea
     *Sowing in the field

2. What did Jesus say he would make the men? (Matthew 4:19)
     *Better fishermen
     *Fishers of men
     *Kind and loving individuals
     *Very wise

3. What did the men do after Jesus called them? (Matthew 4:20)
     *Went back to fishing
     *Went back to sleep
     *Left their nets and went home
     *Left their nets and followed Jesus

4. James and John were in a ship with whom? (Matthew 4:21)
     *Peter and Andrew
     *Zebedee their father
     *Jesus
     *Mary their mother

5. What were James and John doing with their nets? (Matthew 4:21)
     *Fishing with them
     *Throwing them away
     *Buying new ones
     *Mending them

6. Where did Jesus teach? (Matthew 4:23)
    *In the synagogues
    *In the temple
    *In the homes of the people
    *In the churches

7. Throughout which area did Christ's fame go? (Matthew 4:24)
    *Asia
    *Europe
    *Jerusalem
    *Syria

8. Who were brought to Jesus? (Matthew 4:24)
    *All sick people
    *The people who needed salvation
    *All the children
    *Only the disciples

9. When did Jesus come into Galilee preaching the gospel?
    (Mark 1:14)
    *After John was put into prison
    *Before he left Jerusalem
    *After he was old enough
    *After he had called his disciples

10. What did Jesus say was at hand? (Mark 1:15)
    *The time for his death
    *The time to do miracles
    *The fullness of time
    *The kingdom of God

Fishers of Men

These two children are fishers of men, except one is not doing a very good job. Cut out the fish found on page 125 and paste them around the hook of the good fisherman. These fish represent the people to whom we can witness. If you like, when you are finished, you may color the picture.

Please Move -- You're in my Way
Matthew 9:2-8; Mark 2:1-12; Luke 5:17-26

Have you ever stood on a sidewalk and watched a parade march by? They can be very fun, except when someone large is in front of you and you are unable to see anything.

This happened to the men in our lesson for today. They had a friend who could not walk and they wanted to bring him to Jesus to be healed. However, there were so many people crowded into the house where Jesus was, that they could not get in to see Him. So they went up on the flat roof, tore a hole through the clay tiles, and lowered their friend down to the Lord.

It is interesting to understand that these men would not give up. Nothing would keep them from coming to the Lord. They knew that if they could only get to Jesus, everything would be fine.

How important is it for you to get to Jesus and serve Him? Are you willing to stand up to your friends and be good, even if they are doing something bad? Will you sacrifice your time and energy to read your Bible, pray, go to church, and study about the Lord? Or are you just a Christian because your parents or teachers told you this is what you should be?

Like these men, we cannot give up when problems or

trials enter our lives. We need to find a way around them and let nothing stand in the way of our love for the Lord Jesus.

> For I am persuaded, that neither death, nor life, nor angels, nor principalities, nor powers, nor things present, nor things to come, nor height, nor depth, nor any other creature, shall be able to separate us from the love of God, which is in Christ Jesus our Lord. Romans 8:38-39

Read each question and fill in the blanks from the answers in the shaded box on the next page.

1. And behold, they brought to Him a man sick of the
   _____, lying on a _____: and Jesus seeing
   their faith said; Son, be of good cheer; thy _____
   be _____ thee. (Matthew 9:2)

2. When the multitudes saw it, they _____,
   and _____ God, which had given such
   power unto men. (Matthew 9:8)

3. Again He entered into _____ after some
   days; and it was _____ that He was in
   the house. (Mark 2:1)

4. And when they could not come nigh unto him for the press, they uncovered the _____. (Mark 2:4)

5. Certain Scribes reasoned in their hearts, Why doth this man speak _____? Who can forgive sins but _____ alone. (Mark 2:7)

6. Jesus said unto them, why _____ ye these things in your _____? (Mark 2:8)

7. Jesus said, _____, and take up thy bed, and go thy way into thine _____. (Mark 2:11)

8. When Jesus was _____, there were certain _____ and _____ of the law sitting by. (Luke 5:17)

9. The Pharisees and doctors were come out of every town of _____, and _____, and _____. (Luke 5:17)

10. And the people were all _____, and they glorified God, and were filled with _____, saying, We have seen _____ things today. (Luke 5:26)

amazed	Galilee	noised
arise	glorified	palsy
bed	God	Pharisees
blasphemies	hearts	reason
Capernaum	house	roof
doctors	Jerusalem	sins
fear	Judea	strange
forgiven	marvelled	teaching

Please Move -- You're in my Way

Color in these spaces to find what Jesus said to the Pharisees. Read the remaining letters from left to right and write them on the lines in order.

Row A - 1, 2, 5, 7, 8, 9	Row F - 2, 3, 5, 8, 9
Row B - 2, 3, 6, 8, 9	Row G - 1, 2, 5, 6, 9
Row C - 4, 6, 7, 9	Row H - 3, 4, 5, 7, 8, 9
Row D - 1, 4, 5, 6, 7	Row I - 1, 5, 7, 8, 9
Row E - 1, 5, 8	Row J - 1, 2, 3, 4, 5, 6, 7, 8

	A	B	C	D	E	F	G	H	I	J
1	T	I	S	E	O	A	Y	Y	U	F
2	G	N	T	O	Y	I	M	O	U	U
3	R	E	I	S	E	B	A	I	N	O
4	D	T	I	S	A	K	E	G	U	Y
5	Y	P	Y	O	I	M	S	N	T	K
6	O	R	H	T	U	I	I	B	E	N
7	E	D	C	N	A	N	D	I	S	A
8	B	D	G	O	T	A	H	Y	R	H
9	O	L	E	O	M	E	T	D	O	E

___ ___ ___ ___ ___ ___ ___ ___

___ ___ ___ ___ ___ ___ ___ ___

___ ___ ___ ___ ___ ___ ___

___ ___ ___ ___ ___ ___ ___ .

Fantastic Faith
Matthew 8:5-13; Luke 7:1-10

In science class we are taught that we have five senses: our taste, sight, smell, hearing and touch. Most of everything we learn is a result of these senses. We learn to read by hearing and seeing. We learn about food from touching, tasting and smelling. Even our belief in God first comes from hearing the words of Christ in the Bible (Romans 10:17).

Once we hear about the Lord Jesus, we need to have faith in order to believe in Him as our personal Savior. This can be difficult to understand, because faith is something we cannot learn about through our five senses. Hebrews 11:1 says, "Now faith is the assurance of things hoped for, the conviction of things not seen." This means that in order to have faith, we need to believe in the Lord Jesus even though we cannot see Him.

The Centurion believed that his servant would be healed. He trusted the word of the Lord Jesus that he would get better. Do we have that much faith that we can say, "Jesus, I do not need to see you to believe you are God's Son and to know what the Bible teaches about you is true?" The Lord requires us to have this unseeing faith in order to be His children (Ephesians 2:8).

–42–

Fantastic Faith

But without faith it is impossible to please Him: for he that cometh to God must believe that He is, and that He is a rewarder of them that diligently seek Him. Hebrews 11:6

Please indicate your answer with either True or False.

1. _____ Jesus had entered the city of Jerusalem. (Matthew 8:5)

2. _____ The centurion's daughter was sick with the palsy. (Matthew 8:6)

3. _____ The centurion was a man under authority. (Matthew 8:9)

4. _____ Jesus said that the centurion was weak in his faith. (Matthew 8:10)

5. _____ The children of the kingdom shall be cast out into outer darkness. (Matthew 8:12)

6. _____ The elders told Jesus that the centurion had built them a synagogue. (Luke 7:5)

7. _____ The centurion said that he was not worthy for the Lord to enter under his roof. (Luke 7:6)

8. _____ Jesus marvelled when He heard the centurions words. (Luke 7:9)

9. _____ The centurion asked Jesus to say a word to heal his servant. (Luke 7:7)

10. _____ When the elders returned to the house they found that the servant had died. (Luke 7:10)

God's Gift Booklet. Follow the instructions to design a booklet which will remind you of the good things in nature the Lord has given you. The patterns and cut outs are located on page 127, 129 and 131.

Cut cover for booklet (Fig. 1) and color dark blue. Cut out as indicated. Cut sky (Fig. 2) and color light blue and place on inside back cover. Cut sun (Fig. 3) and place on sky; then mountain (Fig. 4); water (Fig. 5); trees (Fig. 6); ground (Fig. 7); and then grass (Fig. 8). Fold the cover (Fig. 1) in half, and staple along the edges (Fig. 9). Note: students may color the pages, or else use them as patterns to cut out colored construction paper.

Fig. 1

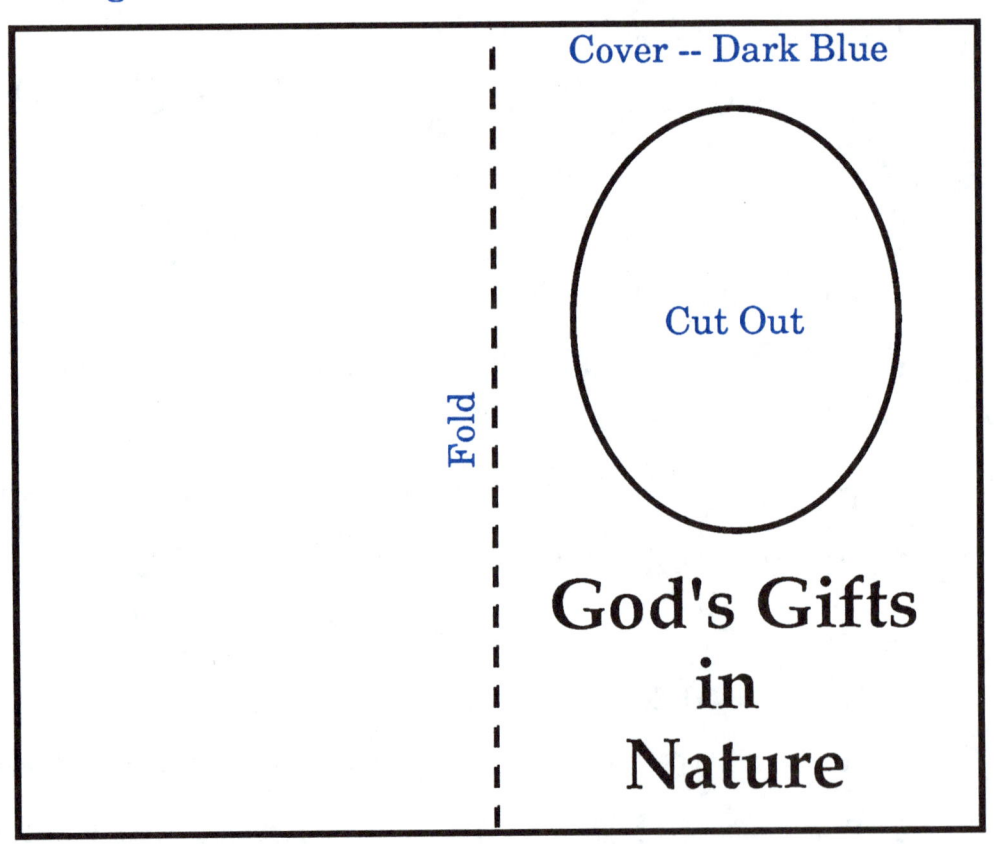

Cover -- Dark Blue

Cut Out

Fold

God's Gifts in Nature

Fig. 2

Sky
Light Blue

The Heavens are thine.
Ps. 89:11

Fig. 9

Staple

God's Gifts in Nature

Fig. 3

Sun
Yellow

*I form the
Light*

Isa. 45:7

Fig. 4

Mountain
Purple

*The mountains
shall bring peace
to the people*

Ps. 72:3

Fig. 5

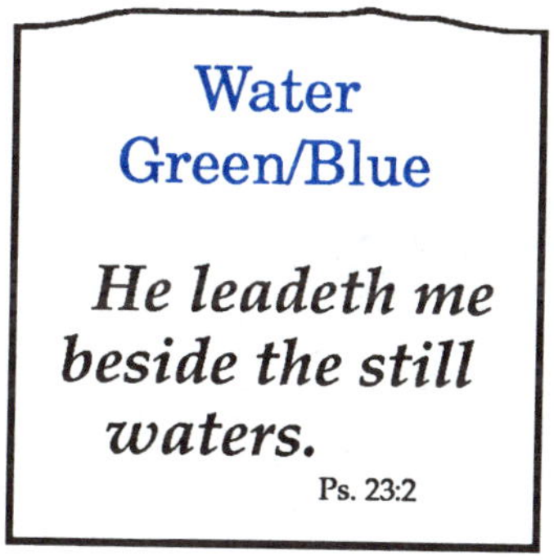

Water
Green/Blue

*He leadeth me
beside the still
waters.*

Ps. 23:2

Fig. 6

Trees
Dark Green

*For the tree is
known by his
fruit.*

Matt. 12:33

Fig. 7

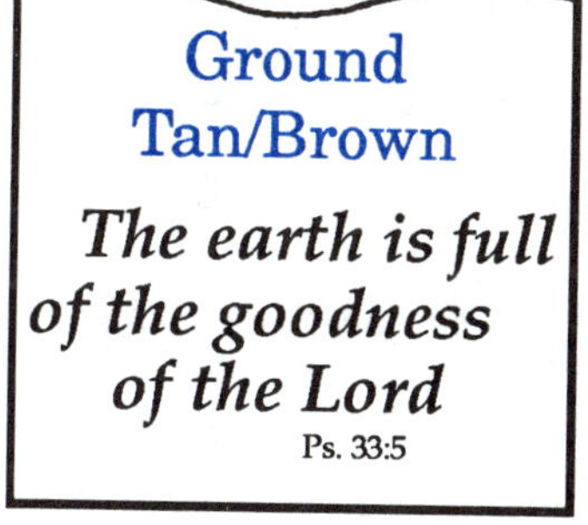

Ground
Tan/Brown

*The earth is full
of the goodness
of the Lord*

Ps. 33:5

Fig. 8

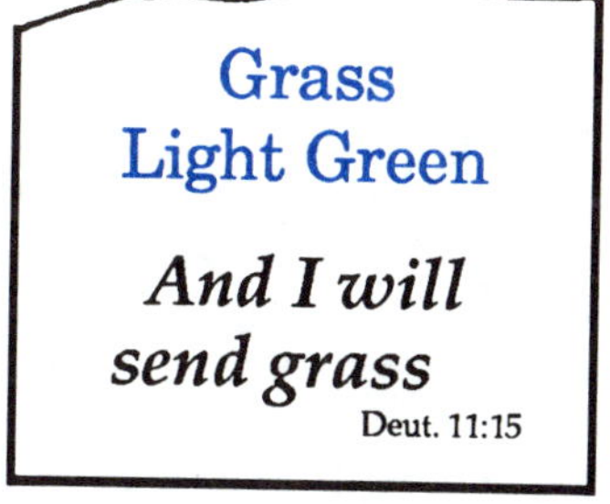

Grass
Light Green

*And I will
send grass*

Deut. 11:15

Peace be Still
Matthew 8:18-27; Mark 4:35-41; Luke 8:22-25

When Jesus calmed the sea, He said, "Peace be still." It is interesting that Jesus used the word "Peace," because as Christians, we are to have peace.

When a person has a peaceful heart, it means that he is not in conflict with anyone. There are three areas where this is true. First of all, a person can have peace with God. In order to do this, he must believe in the Lord Jesus and do what the Bible teaches. Psalm 119:165 says, "Those who love Thy law have great peace, and nothing causes them to stumble.

The next area where we can have peace is with those who are in authority. For most of us, this would mean our parents. When children obey their parents there is no conflict so both are able to live in peace with each other. Ephesians 6:1-2 commands us to obey and honor our father and mother.

Finally, we can have peace with our friends and neighbors by respecting them and being kind to them. Hebrews 12:14 reminds us to pursue peace with all men. This means that we should not purposely do things which aggravate other people, but we should treat them as we would want to be treated ourselves (Matthew 7:12).

Peace is a very important virtue to have, because

without it, life will be miserable for both us and those who are around us. The Lord promises in Philippians 4:6-7 that instead of worrying, we should pray. By giving our concerns over to the Lord we will have peace knowing that God will take care of our problems.

> Thou wilt keep him in perfect peace, whose mind is stayed on thee: because he trusteth in thee. Isaiah 26:3

Color the picture which correctly completes the passage of Scripture.

A certain scribe came and said to Jesus, "Master, I will follow thee wherever you go." And Jesus said to him,

"The [fox] [penguin] have [jeep] [circle] and the [walrus] [bird] of the [clouds] [pear] have [piano] [nest] nests; but the Son of man hath no where to lay His head." (Matthew 8:19-20)

And there arose a great  of wind, and

the  beat into the ship, so that it was

now full. And Jesus was in the hind part of the

 asleep on a pillow; and the disciples

awoke Him, and said, "Master, do you care if we

perish?" And Jesus arose, and rebuked the wind, and

said unto the sea, "Peace be Still." And the wind

ceased, and there was a great calm. (Mark 4:37-39)

And Jesus said to His disciples, "Where is your faith?"

And they being afraid wondered, saying one to

another, "What manner of man is this! For He

commanded even the winds and  , and

they obey Him." (Luke 8:25)

Peace be Still

Read the letters in order and find the one which is missing. Write it on the blank and spell out the answer to this question.

R S U V W X Y Z A............... **T**

A B C D E F G I J............... **H**

D F G H I J K L M............... **E**

T U V X Y Z A B C............... **W**

G H J K L M N O P............... **I**

M O P Q R S T U V............... **N**

A B C E F G H I J............... **D**

X Y Z B C D E F G............... **A**

H I J K L M O P Q............... **N**

V W X Y Z A B C E............... **D**

M N O P Q R S U V............... **T**

F G I J K L M N O............... **H**

C D F G H I J K L............... **E**

Q R T U V W X Y Z............... **S**

D F G H I J K L M............... **E**

S T U V W X Y Z B............... **A**

What obeyed the Lord Jesus?

Attitude Check
Matthew 5:1-7:29

When the Lord Jesus ministered upon the earth, most of His time was spent not doing miracles, but teaching the people how they were to act and think. His message to them was simple: your attitude, or the things which you think, will determine the way you will act; so be careful how you think. Like today, there were many people during that time who felt that God was only interested in their outward actions and not their inward attitudes.

When you are alone, do you think about doing good things or about doing bad things? Is the way you act towards your friends or parents different from the way you think about them? Philippians 4:8 explains that we should think about whatever is true, honorable, right, pure, lovely, good and excellent. This is so that we can develop the same actions. When we think about good things, we will eventually end up doing good things.

Christ called the people who had wicked hearts, white-washed tombs (Matthew 23:27-28). This was because on the outside they looked clean, but on the inside they were full of wickedness. We might be able to fool our friends or teachers into thinking we are good when we have bad thoughts, but we can never fool the Lord Jesus, and eventually everyone will know the truth.

Attitude Check

For man looketh on the outward appearance, but the Lord looketh on the heart. I Samuel 16:7b

Read each question and write the answer from the text for this lesson.

1. How should we let our light shine before men? (Matthew 5:16) ___
   _____

2. What should we do if our brother has something against us? (Matthew 5:24) _____
   _____

3. What should we do if our right hand offends us? (Matthew 5:30)
   _____
   _____

4. What should we do if someone slaps us on our right cheek? (Matthew 5:39) _____

5. How are we to be perfect? (Matthew 5:48) _____
   _____

6. When does our Father know what we need? (Matthew 6:8) _____
   _____

7. Where should we lay our treasure? (Matthew 6:20) _____
   _____

8. What should we seek first? (Matthew 6:33) _____
   _____

9. What is the Law and the Prophets? (Matthew 7:12) _____
   _____

10. Of whom should we beware, and how will we know them? (Matthew 7:15-16) _____
    _____
    _____

Draw a line from one side to the other to correctly complete the sentence. The first one is done for you as an example. This passage of Scripture is called, "The Beatitudes" and is found in Matthew 5:3-12.

Blessed are ...   ## Why

The poor in spirit   They shall inherit
                                      the earth

Those who mourn
                                      They shall be called
                                      the children of God

The meek
                                      Theirs is the kingdom
                                      of heaven
Those who hunger and
thirst after righteousness

                                      They shall see God

The merciful
                                      They shall obtain mercy

The pure in heart
                                      They shall be comforted

The peacemakers
                                      Theirs is the kingdom
                                      of heaven

Those who are persecuted
for righteousness

                                      They shall be filled

Attitude Check

Complete the puzzle by answering the questions. A=Across, D=Down.

- Down -

1. The hypocrites love to stand and pray on these corners. (Matt. 6:5)
2. Blessed are the poor in _____. (Matt. 5:3)
3. Whoever shall break one of these and teach others shall be called least in the kingdom. (Matt 5:19)
5. The hypocrites loved to stand and pray here. (Matt. 6:5)
8. The fowls do not do this. (Matt. 6:26)
11. Your righteousness must exceed that of these people. (Matt. 5:20)

- Across -

4. Who did they persecute? (Matt. 5:12)
6. When you give alms, do not sound this. (Matt. 6:2)
7. For with what judgement ye judge, ye _____ be judged. (Matt. 7:1)
9. All these things shall be _____ unto you. (Matt. 6:33)
10. Beware of false prophets who come to you in this clothing. (Matt. 7:15)
12. Do men gather grapes of _____. (Matt. 7:16)
13. Many will say, Lord did we not do this in your name. (Matt. 7:22)

5000 Hungry Mouths

Matt. 14:13-21; Mark 6:30-44; Luke 9:10-17; John 6:1-14

As we study the life of the Lord Jesus, we are left with a sense of wonder and amazement at the many miracles He performed. From walking on the water to raising the dead, there was nothing Christ could not do.

It is interesting to note that Christ often used people as He did these miracles. It wasn't that He needed their help, but as God, He desired that His children become active in doing good works. When Christ fed the five thousand, He used the five loaves of bread and two fishes from a boy to make enough food for everyone to eat. The Lord did not have to do this. He could have sent His disciples into town to buy enough food for everyone.

As Christians, the Lord has given us all special talents and gifts which we are to use to serve Him. It is not that God needs us to do His work, He is so powerful that He can do anything He chooses. Instead, God uses us that He may be glorified by our good service for Him.

What gifts and talents do you have to bring before the Lord? As you study this lesson, think about the ways you can serve God and show Him obedience and honor.

5000 Hungry Mouths

For it is God which worketh in you both to will and to do of His good pleasure. Philippians 2:13

Match the correct answer with the proper question.

1. _____ How did the people follow Christ? (Matt. 14:13)

2. _____ With what was Jesus moved when He saw the multitude? (Matt. 14:14)

3. _____ Who did Jesus heal? (Matt. 14:14)

4. _____ Jesus compared the people to this kind of animal? (Mark 6:34)

5. _____ How many loaves did the disciples find? (Mark 6:38)

6. _____ How many baskets were left after the people had finished eating? (Mark 6:43)

7. _____ By what city did Jesus take His Apostles? (Luke 9:10)

8. _____ How many fish did the disciples say they had? (Luke 9:13)

9. _____ Of which disciple did Jesus ask where they should buy bread? (John 6:5)

10. ___ How many men did Jesus feed? (John 6:10)

a. Bethsaida

b. Five

c. On foot

d. Sheep

e. Twelve

f. The sick

g. Five thousand

h. Compassion

i. Philip

j. Two

After Christ fed the five thousand, the disciples collected twelve full baskets of left over food. Cut out the pictures on page 133 and paste them onto the baskets. As you work, think about ways you can use these spiritual qualities to serve the Lord. The Scriptures used are Galatians 5:22-26; Ephesians 5:9 and Colossians 1:22.

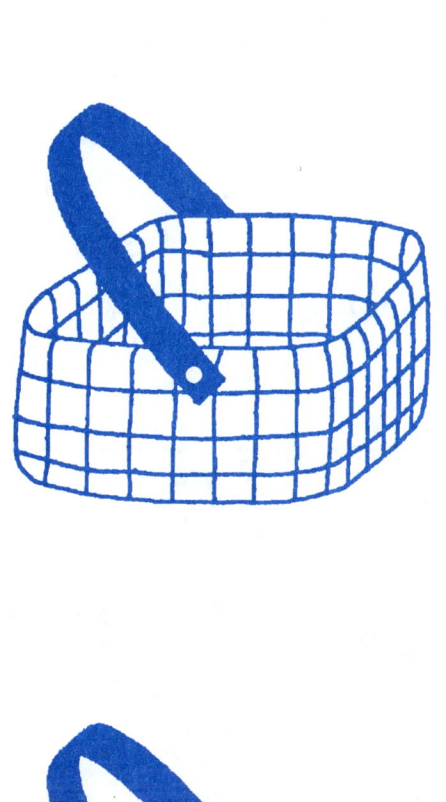
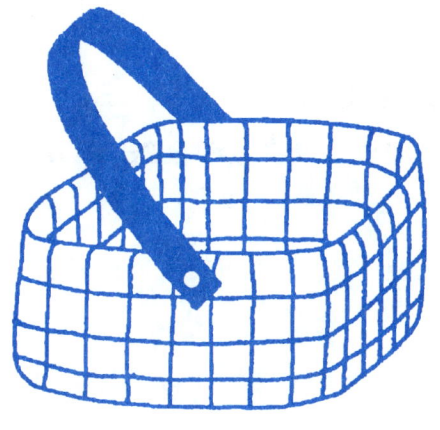
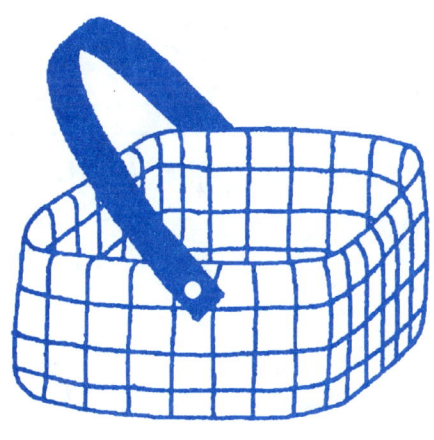
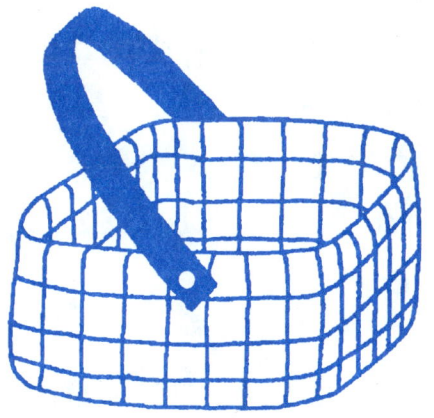
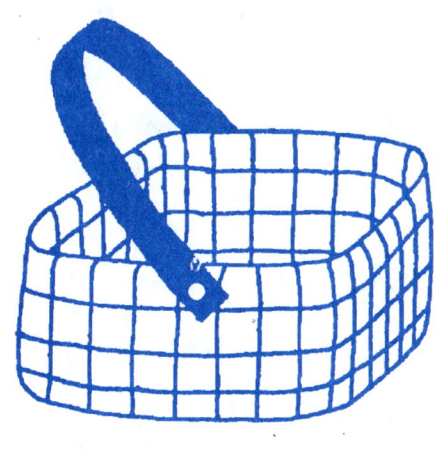
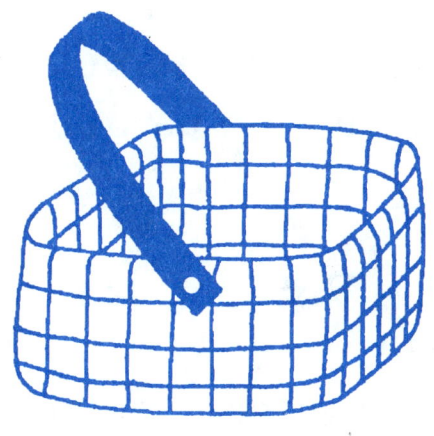

Standing on Faith

Matthew 14:22-33; Mark 6:45-52; John 6:15-21

It is easy to trust the Lord when the sun is shining and things are going good. But what happens when the storm clouds are approaching and there are problems in our lives.

Peter trusted Jesus as long as his attention was focused upon the Savior. However, once he looked around and saw the wind and waves, he became frightened and began to sink. Did Peter  sink into the water because Christ stopped helping him? No! Peter sank because he stopped trusting the Lord.

When we have problems, whether our parents are divorced, or a friend has died, or a bully is after us, or maybe we are very sick, Jesus is there with us. No matter what is wrong, the Lord is helping us to get through the difficulty. When we are afraid and begin to have doubts, we need to look to the Lord and ask Him to help us from sinking into a sea of worry and sin.

Like Peter, if we focus our attention upon our problems and not the Lord Jesus, we will lose our hope and courage. Psalm 46:1 says, "God is our refuge and strength, a very present help in trouble." As we trust the Lord, He will give us the strength to stand and not give up or become fearful in the midst of our trials.

> I will never leave thee, nor forsake thee. Hebrews 13:5b

Multiple choice -- circle the correct answer for each question.

1. What did Jesus constrain His disciples to do? (Matthew 14:22)
    *Get into a ship
    *Feed the 5000
    *Heal the sick
    *Walk on water

2. What did Jesus go up onto the mountain to do? (Matthew 14:23)
    *Heal the sick
    *Talk to the people
    *Pray
    *Sleep

3. Who went out unto the water to meet Jesus? (Matthew 14:29)
    *John
    *Philip
    *James
    *Peter

4. What did Peter cry out? (Matthew 14:30)
    *I'm drowning
    *Pull me out
    *Lord save me
    *Show me how to walk on water

5. What did the disciples think when they saw Jesus walking on the water. (Mark 6:49)
    *That it was a spirit
    *That Jesus had come to save them
    *That they were dreaming
    *That the storm had stopped

6. What did Jesus do when He saw the disciples were troubled?
   (Mark 6:50)
       *He calmed the storm
       *He got into the boat
       *He told Peter to come to Him
       *He talked to them

7. Why didn't the disciples consider the miracle of the loaves?
   (Mark 6:52)
       *They forgot
       *Their hearts were hardened
       *They were to scared
       *They were amazed

8. What did Jesus perceive? (John 6:15)
       *That the people were tired and hungry
       *That He needed to be alone
       *That the people wanted to make Him king
       *That it was getting late in the day

9. Toward which city were the disciples going in their boat?
   (John 6:17)
       *Capernaum
       *Galilee
       *Jerusalem
       *Bethlehem

10. How far had the disciples rowed? (John 6:19)
       *Ten miles
       *300 meters
       *50 furlongs
       *5 and 20 or 30 furlongs

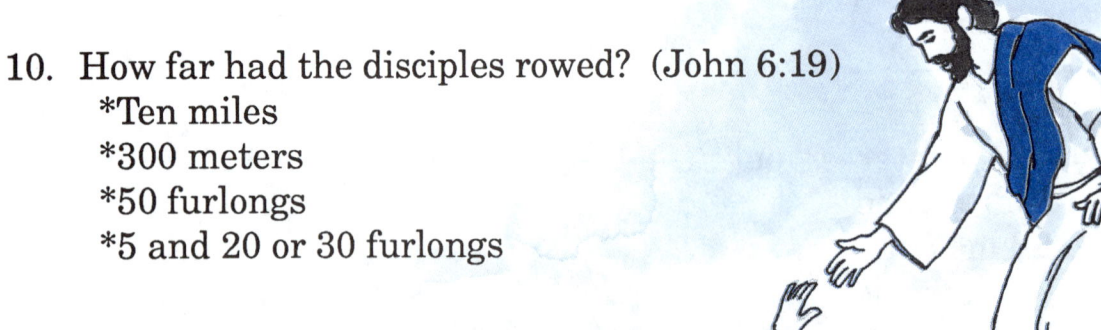

Standing on Faith

Read Matthew 14:22-33, Mark 6:45-52 and John 6:15-21 to complete the crossword puzzle.

- Across -

1. This was hardened. (Mark 6:52)
2. Peter came _____ out of the ship. (Matt. 14:29)
3. The disciples got into this. (Matt. 14:22)
4. Jesus perceived that they would come and _____ Him by force. (John 6:15)
7. When evening had come, the ship was in the _____ of the sea. (Mark 6:47)
10. Jesus stretched this forth and caught Peter. (Matt. 14:31)

- Down -

1. This happened to the disciples' heart. (Mark 6:52)
3. Jesus did this with His hand. (Matt. 14:31)
5. Jesus _____ that they would take Him by force. (John 6:15)
6. When Peter saw the wind _____, he was afraid. (Matt. 14:30)
8. These people went down unto the sea. (John 6:16)
9. The disciples did this while saying, "Of a truth thou art the Son of God." (Matt. 14:33)
11. When did Jesus say, "Be of good cheer: it is I; be not afraid." (Mark 6:50)

The Glory of Christ
Matthew 17:1-13; Mark 9:2-13; Luke 9:28-36

Upon a mountain north of Galilee, the disciples received their first glimpse into the glory of the Lord Jesus Christ. The disciples had difficulty understanding that Christ was God. They knew that He was a very Godly teacher and could do wonderful miracles, but they had not fully comprehended that Jesus was God's Son and an equal member of the Trinity.

Several days earlier, Peter had admitted that Christ was the Son of the living God, (Matthew 16:16). Now the Lord gave him the opportunity to see what his statement truly meant. Before their eyes, Christ was changed as His face shone like the sun and His clothes became white as light.

As we study the lessons of the Lord, we cannot forget that Jesus was both man and God. Philippians 2:6-11, explains that even though Christ was God, He became a man, so that He could suffer and die for our sins. Even as a man He was still God, but He humbled Himself and eventually died on the cross, to pay the penalty for our sins.

During Christ's transfiguration, God the Father spoke from heaven and told us to listen to His Son. Because Jesus is God, we are to obey everything He has taught us in the Bible.

The Glory of Christ

This is my beloved Son, in whom I am well please; hear ye Him. Matthew 17:5b

Read each question and fill in the blanks from the answers in the shaded box on the next page.

1. After six days, Jesus took _____, _____ and _____ his brother, and brought them up into a high _____. (Matthew 17:1)

2. When the disciples heard the voice, they fell on their _____, and were sore _____. And when they lifted up their _____, they saw no man, save Jesus only. (Matthew 17:6-8)

3. When they came down from the mountain, Jesus _____ them saying, tell the _____ to no man, until the _____ of man has _____ from the dead. (Matthew 17:9)

4. And Christ's _____ became shining, exceeding _____ as _____; so as no fuller on _____ can white them. (Mark 9:3)

5. Peter said, _____, it is good for us to be here: and let us make three _____; one for thee and for _____, and one for _____. (Mark 9:5)

6. And there was a cloud that over _____ them: and a _____ came out of the _____, saying, This is my beloved Son: hear Him. (Mark 9:7)

7. And the disciples kept saying with themselves, _____ one with another what the rising from the _____ should mean. (Mark 9:10)

8. Elias verily cometh first, and _____ all things; and how it is written of the Son of man, that He must _____ many things. (Mark 9:12)

9. Moses and Elias _____ in glory, and spake of his _____ which He should accomplish at _____. (Luke 9:31)

10. Peter and they that were with him were heavy with _____: and when they were _____, they saw His _____. (Luke 9:32)

afraid	Elias	Moses	snow
appeared	eyes	mountain	sleep
awake	face	Peter	Son
charged	glory	questioning	suffer
cloud	James	raiment	tabernacles
dead	Jerusalem	restoreth	vision
decease	John	risen	voice
earth	Master	shadowed	white

As we study and obey the Bible, we need to learn the necessary role that it plays in our lives. The following verse is important in this understanding. On the scroll below draw a picture to represent each of the missing words.

Thy _____ is a _____ unto my _____ and a _____ unto my _____ .

Psalm 119:105

Lesson #17

Who is the Greatest
Matthew 18:1-6; Mark 9:33-42; Luke 9:46-48

Children will often argue, "I can hit a ball farther than you," or "I can run faster than you." There is nothing wrong with competition or trying to be the best at something, but when Christ spoke about being great, He wanted us to have a humble attitude.

These days, the world measures the greatness of a person by how well he shoots a basketball or how much money he has. The Bible teaches that if you want to be great in God's Kingdom, you must first be the servant of everyone.

It is not always easy to be a servant; especially if you get an "A" on a test and a fellow classmate got a "D", or if you hit the game winning home run and the player in front of you struck out, or if you just received a new dress, and your friend is still wearing the same skirt she wore last year.

Being a servant means that we will not brag about the things we do. A Godly servant will use his gifts and talents to help other people to excel in what they do. It is important to understand that without God, we could not do anything. Paul says in II Corinthians 10:17, that if we are going to boast, we should boast in the Lord. Since God has given us our life and salvation, we should praise Him and not ourselves for the good things which happen.

Who is the Greatest

When we look at greatness in this way, we can be servants to other people because we are all children of the Lord Jesus.

> Whosover therefore shall humble himself as this little child, the same is greatest in the kingdom of heaven. Matthew 18:4

Please indicate your answer with either True or False.

1. _____ The disciples came to Jesus and asked if He would do more miracles. (Matt. 18:1)

2. _____ Jesus called a child unto Him. (Matt. 18:2)

3. _____ Whoever offended a child it would be better if he were hung with a rope. (Matt. 18:6)

4. _____ The disciples disputed among themselves as to who should be the greatest. (Mark 9:34)

5. _____ Jesus sat down and called the fourteen unto himself. (Mark 9:35)

6. _____ Jesus said, whoever receives a little child in my name, receives me. (Mark 9:37)

7. _____ Peter said that they saw one casting out devils in thy name. (Mark 9:38)

8. _____ He who is not against us is on our part. (Mark 9:40)

9. _____ Whoever shall give you a cup of water because you belong to me shall be punished. (Mark 9:41)

10. ___ Jesus said that he who is least among you shall be least. (Luke 9:48)

Look at the pictures of the children doing good things. They are being kind servants as they help around the house and do their chores. In the space next to each picture write a word or two describing what the child or children are doing.

_____

_____

_____

_____

_____

_____

_____

_____

Who is the Greatest

_____

_____

_____

_____

_____

_____

_____

_____

Forgiveness
Matthew 18:15-35

The Lord Jesus taught us many lessons in the Gospels, but one of the most important is the lesson on forgiveness. We all have been hurt by people in the past. Whether it be a physical hurt like getting beat up by a bully, or an emotional hurt like being misunderstood by our parents, the pain we suffer sometimes takes a long time to go away.

The Lord teaches that we need to forgive those who hurt us. We are not to get angry, bitter or think of ways to get even. We are to forgive that person from our heart and do what we can to help him.

Think about the many times we sin against the Lord Jesus by being disobedient to His Word. Every time we are bad, it offends God. He died on the cross for our sins and wants us to be good. When we sin, we are saying in our hearts that we love ourselves more than we love Jesus.

When we are bad, does God then stop loving us? No! The Lord Jesus forgave our sins when He died on the cross. He will forgive us every time we confess our sins and admit to Him the wrong things we have done.

Since the Lord Jesus forgives us for the terrible things we do every day, we should also be willing to forgive the people who hurt us. By forgiving, we are showing to others the same type of love that Jesus has given to us.

If we confess our sins, He is faithful and just to forgive us our sins, and to cleanse us from all unrighteousness. I John 1:9

Match the correct answer with the proper question.

1. _____ How many times did Peter suggest that he should forgive his brother? (Matt. 18:21)

2. _____ How many times did Jesus say we should forgive our brother? (Matt. 18:22)

3. _____ How many talents did the servant owe the king? (Matt. 18:24)

4. _____ What did the lord command should happen to the servant? (Matt. 18:25)

5. _____ With what was the lord moved ? (Matt. 18:27)

6. _____ What did the lord forgive the servant? (Matt. 18:27)

7. _____ How many pence did the one servant owe the other servant? (Matt. 18:28)

8. _____ Where did the servant cast his fellow servant? (Matt. 18:30)

9. _____ To whom did the lord deliver the servant? (Matt. 18:34)

10. ____ For what are we to forgive our brothers? (Matt. 18:35)

a. He should be sold

b. His debt

c. Their trespass

d. Seventy times seven

e. Tormentors

f. Ten thousand

g. Compassion

h. Seven

i. One hundred

j. Prison

Find and circle the words listed in the word search puzzle. Words may be forward, backward, horizontal, vertical or diagonal.

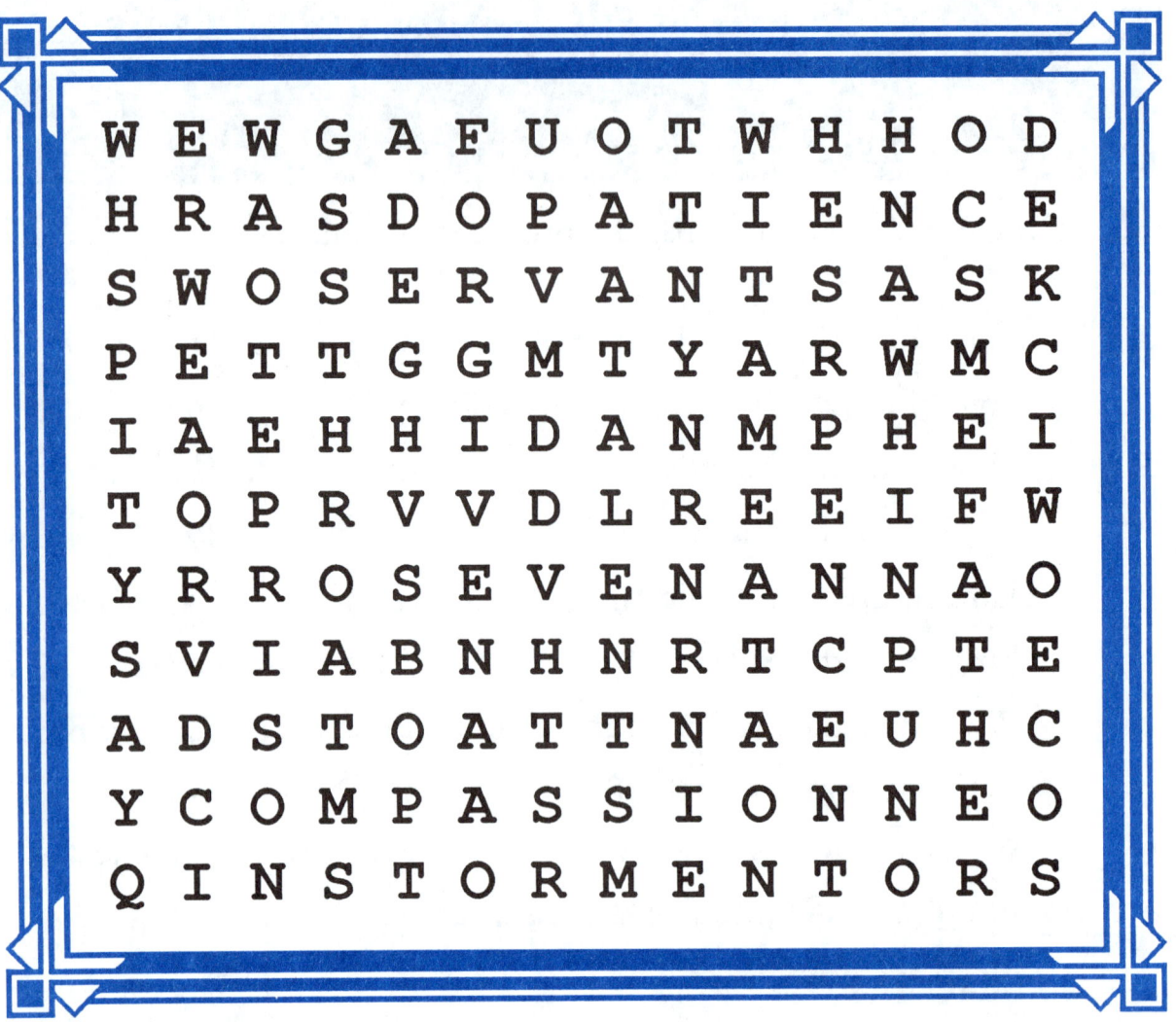

```
W E W G A F U O T W H H O D
H R A S D O P A T I E N C E
S W O S E R V A N T S A S K
P E T T G G M T Y A R W M C
I A E H H I D A N M P H E I
T O P R V V D L R E E I F W
Y R R O S E V E N A N N A O
S V I A B N H N R T C P T E
A D S T O A T T N A E U H C
Y C O M P A S S I O N N E O
Q I N S T O R M E N T O R S
```

COMPASSION	PAYMENT	SORRY
DEBT	PENCE	TALENTS
FATHER	PITY	THROAT
FORGIVE	PRISON	TORMENTORS
HEARTS	SERVANTS	WICKED
PATIENCE	SEVEN	WROTH

Forgiveness

Color in these spaces to find what Jesus said He to the Pharisees. Read the remaining letters from left to right and write them on the lines in order.

Row A - 2, 5, 7	Row F - 3, 7
Row B - 3, 6, 8	Row G - 1, 6, 8
Row C - 1, 5, 7, 9	Row H - 4, 6
Row D - 1, 2, 3, 4	Row I - 2, 5, 7, 9
Row E - 1, 4, 5,	Row J - 1, 5

	A	B	C	D	E	F	G	H	I	J
1	I	F	E	B	O	Y	C	O	U	Y
2	M	F	O	E	R	G	I	V	S	E
3	M	H	E	H	N	A	T	H	E	I
4	R	S	I	T	I	N	S	T	Y	O
5	I	U	T	R	T	H	E	A	S	N
6	V	S	E	N	L	Y	G	E	F	A
7	F	T	O	H	E	R	R	W	C	I
8	L	R	L	A	L	S	E	O	F	O
9	R	G	A	I	V	E	Y	O	D	U

__ __ __ __ __ __ __ __ __ __

__ __ __ __ __ __ __ __ __ __

__ __ __ __ __ __ __ __ __

__ __ __ __ __ __ __ __ __ __

__ __ __ __ __ __

The Good Shepherd
John 10:1-21

Sheep are most interesting animals, but they are also very stupid. Unless sheep have a shepherd, they would wander away from the fold and get themselves eaten by a wild beast.

The Bible compares people to sheep because when it comes to spiritual things, we are very stupid. If we did not have a shepherd to guide and protect us, we would be destroyed by the sin and wickedness which is in the world.

Many times in the Bible, the Lord Jesus is called the "Good Shepherd" (Is. 40:11; Heb. 13:20; I Peter 5:4). This is because He leads and protects His people like a shepherd would guide his sheep. John 10:11 says that the Good Shepherd lays down His life for His sheep. This is what God did for us when He died on the cross. He sacrificed His life so that we could have eternal life.

As you study this lesson, please keep in mind that our role as Christians is to trust our Shepherd. We may not know where the Lord is leading us, but we can trust Him to take care of us.

> I am the good shepherd: the good shepherd giveth His life for the sheep. John 10:11

The Good Shepherd

Fill in the missing letter in each circle from the story of the Good Shepherd. All passages are taken from John 10:1-21.

He that $\bigcirc$ntereth not by the door in the $\bigcirc$heepfold, but climbeth up some other way, the same is a $\bigcirc$hief and a robber. But he that entereth in by the $\bigcirc$oor is the shepherd of the sheep. (10:1-2)

When he putteth forth his own $\bigcirc$heep, he goeth before them, and the sheep follow him: for they know his $\bigcirc$oice. And a $\bigcirc$tranger they will not $\bigcirc$ollow, but will flee from him: for they know not the voice of strangers. (10:4-5)

Jesus said, I am the door: by me if any man enter in, he shall be $\bigcirc$aved, and shall go in and out, and find $\bigcirc$asture. (10:9)

I am come that they might have $\bigcirc$ife, and that they might have it more $\bigcirc$bundantly. (10:10)

I am the $\bigcirc$ood shepherd: the good shepherd giveth his life for the $\bigcirc$heep. (10:11)

As the Father knoweth me, even so know I the Father:

and I lay down my life for the sheep. (10:15)

Therefore doth my ◯ather love me, because I lay down my life, that I might ◯ake it again. No man taketh it from me, but I lay it down of myself. I have power to lay it down, and I have ◯ower to take it again. (10:17-18)

And many of them said ◯esus, he hath a devil, and is ◯ad; why hear ye him? Others said, these are not the words of him that hath a devil. Can a devil open the eyes of the ◯lind? (10:20-21)

Complete the vertical crossword by finding the missing words from the passage of Scripture and filling them in the blank squares. There is a secret message in the middle boxes, can you find it?

John 10:9-16
[1] am the door: by me if any man enter in, he shall be [2], and shall go in and out, and find [11]. The thief [3] not, but for to steal, and to kill, and to [4]: I am come that they might have [6], and that they might have it more abundantly. I am the good shepherd: the good shepherd [7] his life for the sheep. But he that is an hireling, and not the shepherd, whose [8] the sheep are not, seeth the [9] coming, and leaveth the sheep, and fleeth: and the wolf catcheth them, and scattereth the sheep. The hireling fleeth, because he is an [12], and [13] not for the sheep. I am the [10] [14], and know my [5], and am known of mine. As the Father knoweth me, even so know I the [15]: and I lay down my life for the sheep. And other [16] I have, which are not of this fold: them also I must [17], and they shall hear my voice; and there shall be one [18], and one shepherd.

The Good Shepherd

The Good Samaritan
Luke 10:25-37

A few lessons back, we learned the importance of forgiving those who wrong us. Now imagine that the person who has hurt us the most is in trouble and in need of help. How should we act toward that person? In order to be a good Samaritan, we are to help that individual even if it means we could be hurt in the process.

When Jesus told the people this parable, He was explaining to them that we are to love our neighbor just as much as we love ourselves. This means when someone is in trouble, we should do all we can to help him.

Did you notice in the parable that the Priest and Levite, **two religious people whom you would expect to** help someone, simply ignored the injured man. It took a Samaritan, (an enemy of the Jews), to offer the hurting person safety and shelter.

It is easy for us to be kind and helpful to people who  are nice to us. However, Jesus said our neighbor is anyone who needs our help. Starting today, try to find ways we can be "Good Samaritans" and help people. Especially those who have not been nice to us in the past.

The Good Samaritan

Read each question and write the answer from the text for this lesson.

1.   Who tempted Jesus? (Luke 10:25) _____

2.   How should you love your neighbor? (Luke 10:27) _____
_____

3.   A certain man went down from Jerusalem to where? (Luke 10:30)
_____

4.   Of what did the thieves strip the man? (Luke 10:30) _____
_____

5.   What did the priest do when he saw the man? (Luke 10:31) _____
_____

6.   What did the Samaritan pour on the man's wounds? (Luke 10:34)
_____

7.   Where did the Samaritan bring the man? (Luke 10:34) _____
_____

8.   How much did the Samaritan give to the host to take care of the man? (Luke 10:35) _____

9.   Who did Jesus say the man fell among? (Luke 10:36) _____
_____

10. Who did the lawyer say was the neighbor to the hurt man? (Luke 10:37) _____
_____

Studying God's Word Book D

Decode the symbols to understand the secret message. The key is in the box at the side of this page.

LOVE THE

LORD WITH

ALL THY

HEART, SOUL,

STRENGTH,

AND MIND.

LUKE 10:27

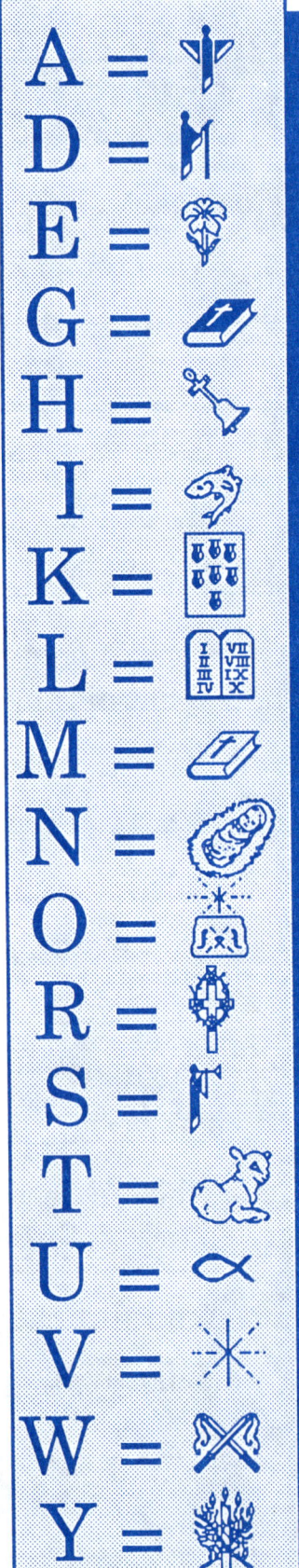

Key:

A =
D =
E =
G =
H =
I =
K =
L =
M =
N =
O =
R =
S =
T =
U =
V =
W =
Y =

The Good Samaritan

Review is important so that we do not forget the things that we have learned. Draw a line from the person or event to the picture it represents.

BIRTH OF CHRIST

WISE MEN BRING
CHRIST GIFTS

CHRIST'S BAPTISM

CHRIST TALKS WITH
WOMAN AT THE WELL

LAME MAN HEALED
BY POOL

MAN LET DOWN
THROUGH ROOF

FAITH OF THE
CENTURION

FEEDING THE 5000

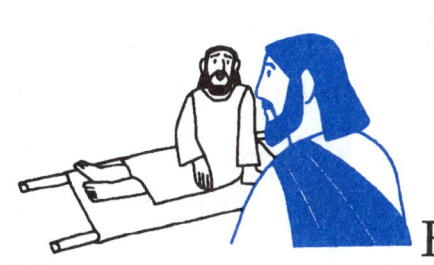

Heavenly Treasure Chest
Luke 12:13-34

Do you ever wonder what it would be like to have so much money that you could not spend it all? Jesus taught us that we are to put our trust in Him and not in the riches of the world. The rich man in this lesson thought money could save him; he was wrong. When he died, he went to hell because he did not trust in God.

The Bible teaches that if we love money or things more than we love God, we are sinning (Matthew 6:24; I Timothy 6:10). God will sometimes bless people with riches, but we are not to seek after them. We are to use our money to help people and be righteous.

Years ago, pirates would bury the treasure they stole in places where no one could find it. They did not have banks in which to keep their riches, so they would hide them and draw maps to find them again. This is what is meant by laying up treasure on the earth, taking money and not doing anything good with it.

Christ wants us to lay up our treasure in heaven. By doing good things and taking our money to help people, we will be rewarded by God in heaven. God does not want us to be selfish with the things we have. He wants us to share with others. In the eyes of God, we are rich when we share the good things He has given us with those who are in need.

Heavenly Treasure Chest

> But lay up for yourselves treasures in heaven, where neither moth nor rust doth corrupt, and where thieves do not break through nor steal. Matthew 6:20

Each of the pictures below has something to do with the temptation of Christ. Match up the correct Scripture reference with each picture. All passages are taken from Luke 12:13-34.

12:17   12:18   12:24

12:27   12:30   12:33

In the chests are treasures we can store up in heaven. Look up the Bible verses, unscramble the words and write them in the blanks below.

Ephesians 6:2

OORNH

_____ YOUR FATHER AND YOUR MOTHER

II Timothy 4:2

RPHCAE

_____ THE WORD, BE READY IN SEASON AND OUT OF SEASON

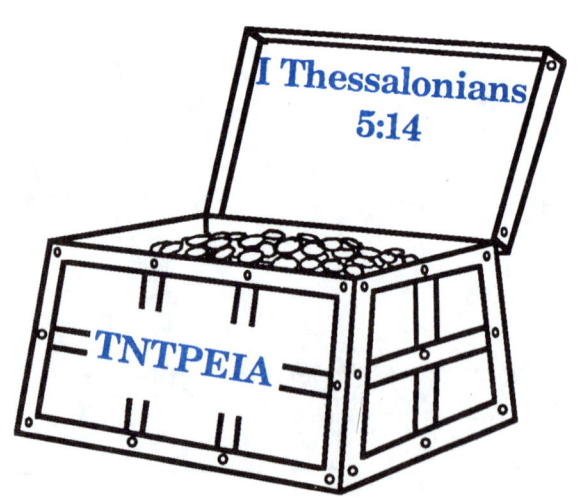

I Thessalonians 5:14

TNTPEIA

BE _____ TOWARD ALL MEN

James 5:16

PYRREA

THE EFFECTIVE _____ OF A RIGHTEOUS MAN CAN ACCOMPLISH MUCH

Heavenly Treasure Chest

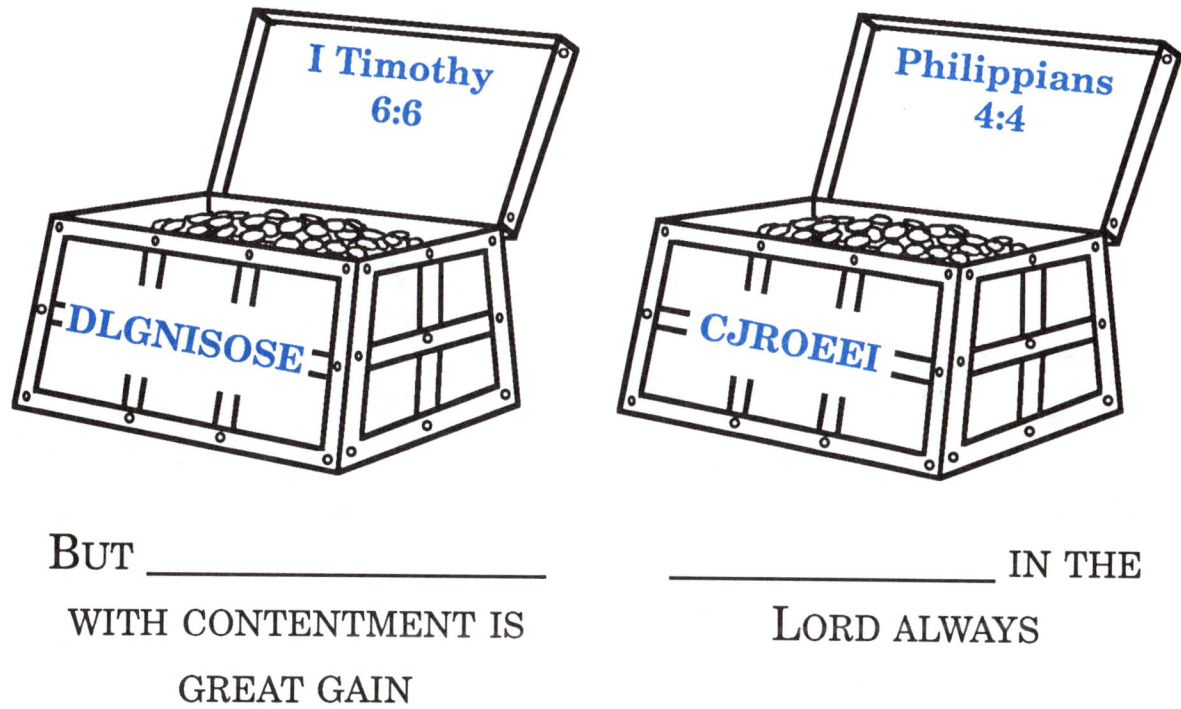

I Timothy 6:6

DLGNISOSE

Philippians 4:4

CJROEEI

BUT _____

WITH CONTENTMENT IS

GREAT GAIN

_____ IN THE

LORD ALWAYS

Now if any man builds upon the foundation with gold, silver, precious stones, wood, hay, straw, each man's work will become evident, because it is to be revealed with fire. If any man's work which he has built upon it remains, he shall receive a reward. I Corinthians 3:12-14

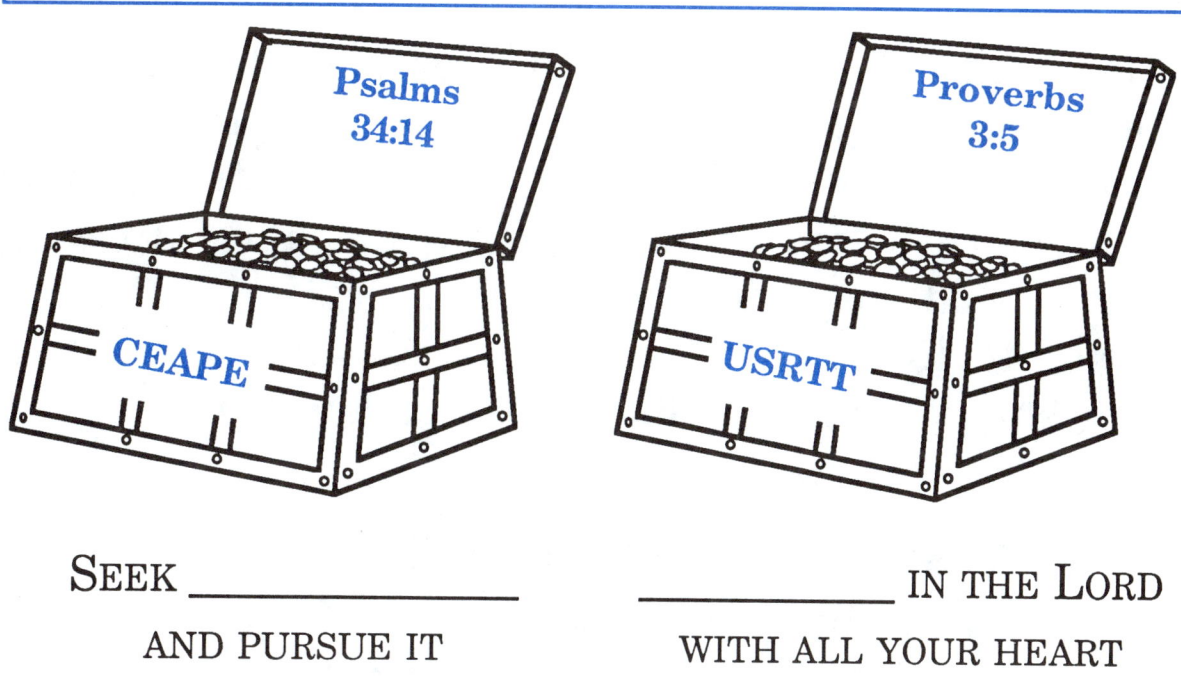

Psalms 34:14

CEAPE

Proverbs 3:5

USRTT

SEEK _____

AND PURSUE IT

_____ IN THE LORD

WITH ALL YOUR HEART

The Prodigal Son
Luke 15:11-32

As children, we do not always do the things our parents tell us. We sin when we disobey them and make them very sad. It hurts our parents when we are bad because they want us to obey God's Word. This is why our parents spank or discipline us, not because they do not love us, but because they love us so much that they want us to be good.

Christians often disobey God and sin against Him. When this happens, like our parents, God will discipline us because He wants us to be holy. Hebrews 12:7 says, "It is for discipline that you endure; God deals with you as with sons; for what son is there whom his father does not discipline?" (NASV)

After we are disciplined and repent of our sin, the Lord Jesus restores us in fellowship with Him. Like the father of the prodigal son, God wants to welcome us back into His family. When a Christian sins against God, he does not lose his salvation, but he is out of fellowship with the Lord. So when the fellowship is restored, God is pleased and we are again united with our heavenly Father.

> For whom the Lord loveth He chasteneth, and scourgeth every son whom He receiveth. Hebrews 12:6

The Prodigal Son

Please indicate your answer with either True or False.

1. _____ The son went into a far country and invested his money wisely. (Luke 15:13)

2. _____ The son went into the fields to feed swine. (Luke 15:15)

3. _____ The son decided to go back to his father and ask to be made a servant. (Luke 15:19)

4. _____ When the father saw the son he was angry and yelled at him. (Luke 15:20)

5. _____ The father told his servants to put the best robe on his son. (Luke 15:22)

6. _____ When the elder son came to the house, he heard music and dancing. (Luke 15:25)

7. _____ When the son came home, the father killed the fatted bird. (Luke 15:27)

8. _____ The elder brother was happy that his brother had returned home. (Luke 15:28)

9. _____ The elder son told his father that he had never transgressed any of his commands. (Luke 15:29)

10. _____ The father said that his son was dead but now is alive again. (Luke 15:32)

Explain in your own words what is being said in each picture.

What did the son say to his father?	What did the son say to himself?

Luke 15:12	Luke 15:17-19

What did the elder brother
say to his father?

What did the father say to
the elder brother?

Luke 15:29-30

Luke 15:31-32

Eternal Life
John 11:1-57

One of the last major miracles that Christ did before His death was the raising of Lazarus from the dead. Some may wonder, (like Mary and Martha), why Christ did not heal Lazarus before he died? We have already studied that Christ could heal people without even being in their presence. So why didn't He will to make His good friend better immediately?

Many people believe it was because Christ wanted to show that just as he had the power to raise Lazarus from the dead, He also had the power to be resurrected. Christ wanted Lazarus to die so that He could bring him back to life again, and show His power over the grave.

Some day each of us will die, and although we will not get a second chance on life like Lazarus did, we will be resurrected. The Bible is very clear that those who love the Lord Jesus will go to live with Him for eternity, but those who do not believe will perish in hell forever (Psalm 9:17).

Take a look at your life and examine your heart before the Lord. Hopefully each of you have believed in Jesus as your personal Savior. As His children, we do not need to fear death, for Christ has the power to resurrect us to a new life. "Therefore we are buried with Him by baptism into death: that like as Christ was raised up from the dead by the glory of the Father, even so we also should walk in newness of life (Romans 6:4).

> I am the resurrection, and the life: he that believeth in me, though he were dead, yet shall he live. John 11:25

Multiple choice -- circle the correct answer for each question.

1. Why did Jesus say that Lazarus was sick? (John 11:4)
    *That the Son of God may be glorified
    *To teach the people a lesson
    *Because he had sinned
    *So the disciples would know why He had to leave

2. After Jesus heard that Lazarus was sick, how long did He stay where he was? (John 11:6)
    *One week
    *Two days
    *Two weeks
    *One hour

3. Where did Jesus tell his disciples that He was going to go again? (John 11:7)
    *Jerusalem
    *Nazareth
    *Judaea
    *Galilee

4. What did the disciples think Jesus was speaking about? (John 11:13)
    *That Lazarus had died
    *That Lazarus had gotten better
    *That Lazarus was going to come and meet them
    *That Lazarus had taken a rest in sleep

5. How long had Lazarus been dead when Jesus came to him?
    (John 11:17)
    *Three days
    *Two days
    *Four days
    *Four hours

6. What did Martha know? (John 11:22)
    *That Lazarus was dead
    *That Jesus was coming
    *That it was to late to help Lazarus
    *That whatever Jesus asked of God, God would give it to Him

7. Who did Martha say Jesus was? (John 11:27)
    *The resurrection and the life
    *The creator of the world
    *The Christ, the Son of God
    *A very good man

8. What was Martha afraid of if they moved the stone covering the
    grave? (John 11:39)
    *That Lazarus would stink
    *That someone might get hurt
    *That Lazarus would walk out
    *That the people would stop weeping

9. What did the chief priests and Pharisees do from that day forth?
    (John 11:53)
    *Followed after Jesus
    *Counseled together to put Jesus to death
    *Believed in the Lord Jesus
    *Talk to Lazarus about death

10. What commandment did the chief priests and Pharisees give?
    (John 11:57)
    *That if anyone knew where Jesus was, they should show it
    *That the people were to celebrate the passover
    *That everyone was to leave Jesus alone
    *That they were not going to bother Jesus any longer

Eternal Life

The Gospels record many miracles performed by Christ. As a way of review, look up the following passages of Scripture and draw a line connecting them to the correct miracles.

Matthew 8:5-13

Matthew 8:14-17

Matthew 14:13-21

Mark 2:1-12

Mark 6:45-52

Luke 8:22-25

Luke 8:26-33

John 2:1-11

John 5:1-9

John 11:38-44

Jesus turns water into wine

Man by the pool healed

Friends let paralytic down through roof to see Christ

Centurion's servant healed

Jesus calms the sea

Christ feeds the 5000

Jesus walks on the water

Demons cast out of a man

Peter's mother-in-law healed

Raising of Lazarus from the dead

Grateful Living
Luke 17:11-19

Let's stop for a moment to consider all the wonderful things people have done for us in the past. Whether it be our parents, teachers, friends or neighbors, if we think about it, a lot of people have been there to help and guide us. Even God, through the blessings He has given us, has helped us more times than we can count. When was the last time we let these people know how much they mean to us?

When Christ healed the ten lepers, only one came back to say "thank you". The other nine quickly forgot about the miracle that the Lord did for them and left without saying a word.

We sometimes have the tendency to take people for granted. Just because God's law requires our parents and teachers to guide and care for us does not mean that we should come to expect every kind thing which they do. It is not fair to make demands upon people especially when we are unwilling to be kind in return.

Tonight before you go to sleep, besides thanking the Lord Jesus for the wonderful things he has done for you, think of someone who has been kind to you and do something nice for them. Even saying "thank you", in a letter or in person, can go a long way to make someone feel appreciated.

Grateful Living

So we thy people and sheep of thy pasture will give thee thanks for ever: we will shew forth thy praise to all generations. Psalms 79:13

Read each question and write the answer from the text for this lesson.

1. Jesus passed through the midst of what two areas? (Luke 17:11)

    _____

2. Who stood afar off? (Luke 17:12) _____

3. What did the lepers lift up? (Luke 17:13) _____

4. What did the lepers say to Jesus? (Luke 17:13) _____

    _____

5. To whom did Christ tell the lepers to show themselves?

    (Luke 17:14) _____

6. What did the one leper do with a loud voice? (Luke 17:15) _____

    _____

7. Where did the leper fall down? (Luke 17:16) _____

    _____

8. What nationality was the leper? (Luke 17:16) _____

9. What questions did Jesus ask the leper? (Luke 17:17) _____

    _____

    _____

10. What did Jesus say made the leper whole? (Luke 17:19)_____

    _____

Studying God's Word Book D

This crossword puzzle is taken from Psalms 148. Look at the many ways we can praise the Lord and show our thankfulness to Him.

Complete the puzzle by answering the questions. A=Across, D=Down.

- Across -

2. For the Lord _____ and they were created. (148:5)
5. _____ ye the Lord (148:1)
6. Praise Him, ye ____ of ____. (148:4)
8. He hath also ____ them forever. (148:6) [Use NKJV. See note below.]
11. Another name for cow. (148:10)
12. Name for young kings. (148:11)

(Note: #8 Across is "established" [NKJV].)

- Down -

1. A kind of tree. (148:9)
2. When God made the world. (148:5)
3. Very big hills. (148:9)
4. A nation. (148:14)
6. Praise the Lord in the _____. (148:1)
7. This is above the heaven and earth. (148:13)
9. Name for good people. (148:14)
10. A _____ near unto Him. (148:14)

Grateful Living

Read the letters in order and find the one which is missing. Write it on the blank and spell out the answer to this question.

A C D E F G H I J . . . . _____

Y Z A B C D F G H . . . . _____

D E F H I J K L M . . . . _____

M N O P Q S T U V . . . . _____

T U V W X Y Z B C . . . . _____

Q R S U V W X Y Z . . . . _____

D F G H I J K L M . . . . _____

A B C D E G H I J . . . . _____

S T V W X Y Z A B . . . . _____

J K M N O P Q R S . . . . _____

N O P Q R S U V W . . . . _____

G H I J K L M N P . . . . _____

U V W X Y Z B C D . . . . _____

F G H I J K M N O . . . . _____

K M N O P Q R S T . . . . _____

How are we to act?

_____

Outward Appearances
Luke 19:1-10

I have always enjoyed the story of Zacchaeus because like him, I too am short. When I went to school, the other kids would sometimes call me names like shorty, half-pint and midget. So whenever I would read about Zacchaeus, it gave me confidence knowing that if this short man could serve the Lord, then I could too.

As I grew older, I came to understand that God made each of us different in order to serve Him in various ways. We may be short or tall, fat or skinny. We may have big ears and a flat nose or red hair with freckles. Regardless of how we appear, what really is important is the attitude of our heart.

Ephesians 1:4 says that God chose us before the foundation of the world. This means that even before God created the heavens and earth, He had each of us in mind and knew what we would do and look like.

If there is something about yourself that you think God would like to see improved, then try to change it. For example, if you stutter, take speech lessons. However, if you can't do anything about the way you are, like being short, then work on your attitude.

If you feel bad about the way you were created, just remember the saying, "I'm somebody special, because God doesn't make any junk." Each of us is special because God, in His perfect wisdom, chose to make us exactly the way we are.

According as He hath chosen us in Him before the foundation of the world, that we should be holy and without blame before Him in love. Ephesians 1:4

Read each question and fill in the blanks from the answers in the shaded box on the next page.

1. _____ entered and passed through _____. (Luke 19:1)

2. There was a man named _____, which was the _____ among the _____, and he was rich. (Luke 19:2)

3. Zacchaeus sought to see Jesus, and could not for the _____, because he was little of _____. (Luke 19:3)

4. He climbed up into a _____ tree to see him, for he was to _____ that way. (Luke 19:4)

5. Jesus said to Zacchaeus, make haste and come _____; for to day I must _____ at thy _____. (Luke 19:5)

6. He made haste and came down and _____ Jesus _____. (Luke 19:6)

7. When the people saw this they _____, that Jesus was gone to be _____ with a man that is a _____. (Luke 19:7)

8. Zacchaeus told Jesus that _____ his goods he would give to the _____, and if he had taken any thing from any man by false _____, he would _____ him _____. (Luke 19:8)

9. This day is _____ come to this house, for Zacchaeus is a son of _____. (Luke 19:9)

10. For the Son of _____ is come to _____ and to _____ that which was _____. (Luke 19:10)

abide	half	murmured	salvation
Abraham	house	pass	save
accusation	Jericho	poor	seek
chief	Jesus	press	sinner
down	joyfully	publicans	stature
fourfold	lost	received	sycamore
guest	man	restore	Zacchaeus

I believe Jesus died for me.

Outward Appearances

Help Zacchaeus find a tree so he can climb up and see Jesus.

Triumphal Entry

Matt. 21:1-11; Mark 11:1-11; Luke 19:29-44; John 12:12-19

A week before the people in Jerusalem condemned Christ to death, they were honoring Him as their King. This seems a little strange, but it just goes to show that many people did not understand the message Christ was teaching them (John 12:16). Whereas, they thought Jesus had come as their King to free them from the Romans, He really came to Jerusalem as a servant to die for the sins of His people.

Looking back at this now, we can see that dying for our sins was the most important sacrifice Christ could make. Unfortunately, the people did not want a Savior, they wanted a soldier. They were not willing to come to God and serve Him, instead they wanted the Lord to serve them.

Sometimes we act like the people in Jerusalem. All we say to God is: give me this or give me that, or help me here or protect me there; when what we should be praying is: God, how can I serve you?

Just as Jesus wept over Jerusalem, He longs for us to follow Him. It is our duty to serve the Lord and not to think only of our own interests. Let us try to avoid the selfish habit of always asking for something from God, and instead give Him our service and love.

Triumphal Entry

Match the correct answer with the proper question.

1. _____ Who did Jesus send to find a colt? (Matt. 21:1)

2. _____ What did the disciples put on the colt? (Matt. 21:7)

3. _____ What did the multitude spread in the way? (Matt. 21:8)

4. _____ Where did the disciples find the colt tied? (Mark 11:4)

5. _____ What did the people straw in the way? (Mark 11:8)

6. _____ What did the people cry out when Jesus went by? (Mark 11:9)

7. _____ Where did Jesus go after He looked around Jerusalem? (Mark 11:11)

8. _____ What did Jesus say would cry out, if the disciples held their peace? (Luke 19:40)

9. _____ What did Jesus do when He beheld the city? (Luke 19:41)

10. _____ Who did the Pharisees say had gone after Jesus? (John 12:19)

a. By the door

b. The stones

c. Their garments

d. Two disciples

e. Wept

f. Branches

g. The world

h. Their clothes

i. Hosanna

j. Bethany

Jesus Pilot Me Booklet. Follow the instructions to design a booklet which will remind you of the good things in nature the Lord has given you. The patterns and cut outs are located on pages 135 and 137.

Cut cover for booklet (Fig. 1) and color light brown. Cut out cross as indicated. Cut sky (Fig. 2) and color light blue and place on inside back cover. Cut sun (Fig. 3) and place on sky; cut ship (Fig. 4); water (Fig. 5); and then land (Fig. 6). Fold the cover (Fig. 1) in half, and staple along the edges (Fig. 7). Note: students may color the pages, or else use them as patterns to cut out colored construction paper.

Fig. 1

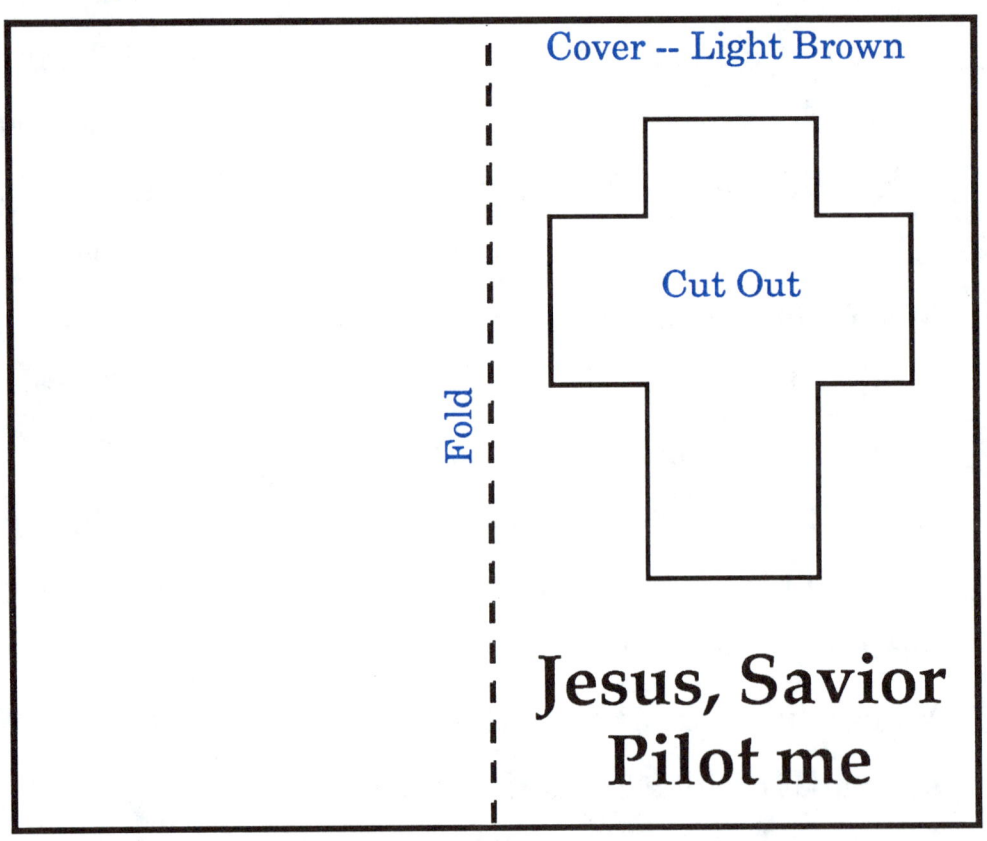

Cover -- Light Brown

Cut Out

Fold

Jesus, Savior
Pilot me

Fig. 2

Sky
Light Blue

*Jesus, Savior
pilot me*

Fig. 7

Staple

Jesus, Savior
Pilot me

Fig. 3

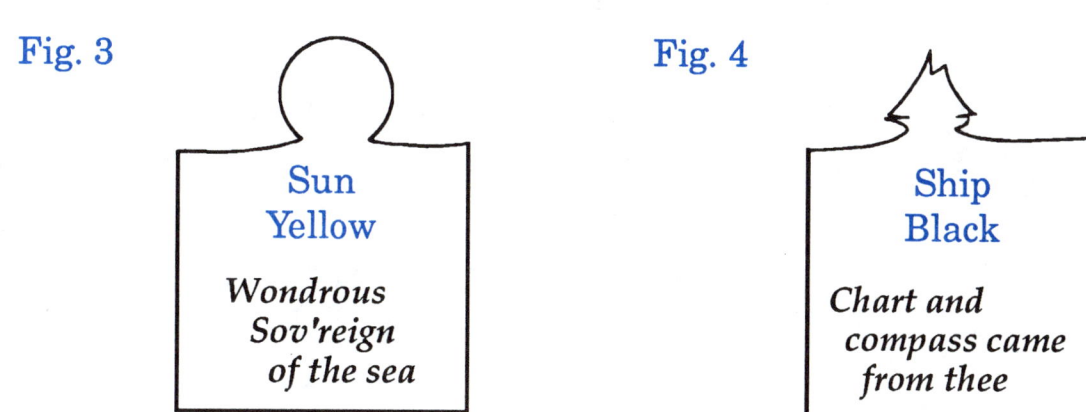

Sun
Yellow

*Wondrous
Sov'reign
of the sea*

Fig. 4

Ship
Black

*Chart and
compass came
from thee*

Fig. 5

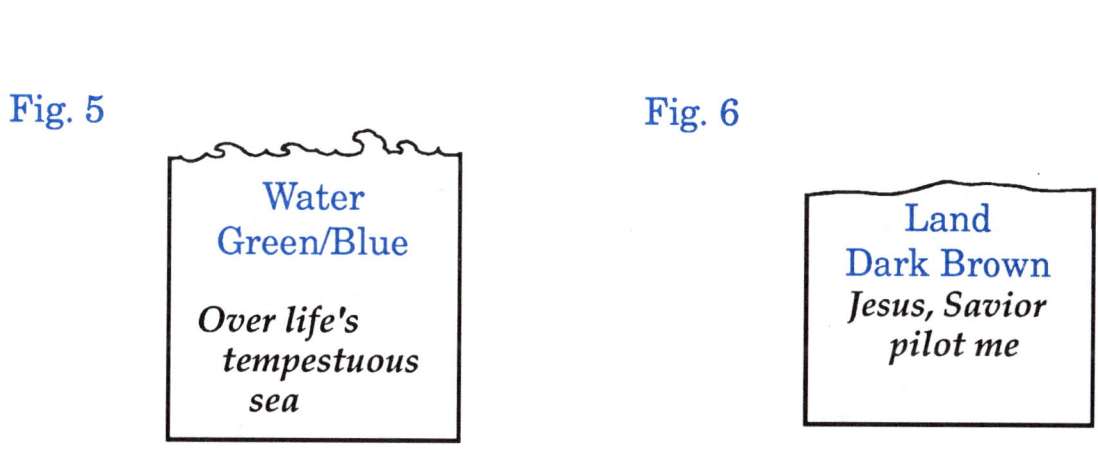

Water
Green/Blue

*Over life's
tempestuous
sea*

Fig. 6

Land
Dark Brown
*Jesus, Savior
pilot me*

Peter Denies Christ

Matt. 26:69-75; Mark 14:66-72; Luke 22:54-62; John 18:15-27

As Christians, we need to be willing to stand up for our faith in the Lord Jesus no matter what may happen to us. Whether at home, school or just around the neighborhood, God wants us to tell other people about Him.

It is sometimes difficult to admit to people that we are Christians. We tend to act ashamed because we are afraid of what other people may think about us if we are different. Look at what happened to Peter. He had been with Christ for three years and had promised that he would never deny the Lord (Matt. 26:33-34). However, when his faith was put to the test, he told the people that he never even knew Jesus.

We need to realize that it is far more important what the Lord thinks about us, then it is what people think. Paul wrote in Romans 1:16, that he was not ashamed of the Gospel. The Apostle understood that people were only saved by believing in the Lord Jesus, and he was going to do everything he could to tell them about this. People may not agree with you or like the things you say, but that is no excuse not to talk about the Lord.

Peter Denies Christ

Whosoever therefore shall confess me before men, him will I confess also before my Father which is in heaven. But whosoever shall deny me before men, him will I also deny before my Father which is in heaven. Matthew 10:32-33

Multiple choice -- circle the correct answer for each question.

1. Where was Peter when another maid spoke to him? (Matt. 26:71)
   *In the palace
   *By the temple
   *On the porch
   *In the garden

2. What did the people say betrayed Peter? (Matt. 26:73)
   *The other disciples
   *Jesus
   *The high priest
   *His speech

3. What did Peter remember? (Matt. 26:75)
   *The word of Jesus
   *The time of day
   *All the miracles which Jesus performed
   *Where the other disciples were

4. Who did the maid say was with Peter? (Mark 14:67)
   *The other disciples
   *Mary and Martha
   *Jesus of Nazareth
   *John the Baptist

5. What did the maid say Peter was? (Mark 14:70)
   *A Galilean
   *A fisherman
   *A disciples
   *A trouble maker

6. What did the Lord turn and do? (Luke 22:61)
   *He spoke to the crowd
   *He looked at Peter
   *He spoke to Peter
   *He cried

7. What did Peter go out and do after he denied the Lord?
   (Luke 22:62)
   *Hung himself
   *Went fishing
   *He found the other disciples
   *Wept bitterly

8. By whom was the other disciple known? (John 18:15)
   *Barabbas
   *Pontius Pilate
   *The high priest
   *A young damsel

9. What did the high priest ask Jesus about? (John 18:19)
   *If he was the Son of God
   *If Peter was His disciple
   *How he could do so many wonderful miracles
   *His disciples and His doctrine

10. Who struck Jesus with the palm of his hand? (John 18:22)
    *Annas
    *Caiaphas
    *One of the officers
    *Peter

Peter Denies Christ

A good way to learn a Bible verse is to take it apart and put it together again from memory. Cut out the puzzle pieces on page 139 and fit them into the correct spaces on the house. Practice saying the verse several times as you put it together. Try not to look at the verse in Romans until you have it all finished.

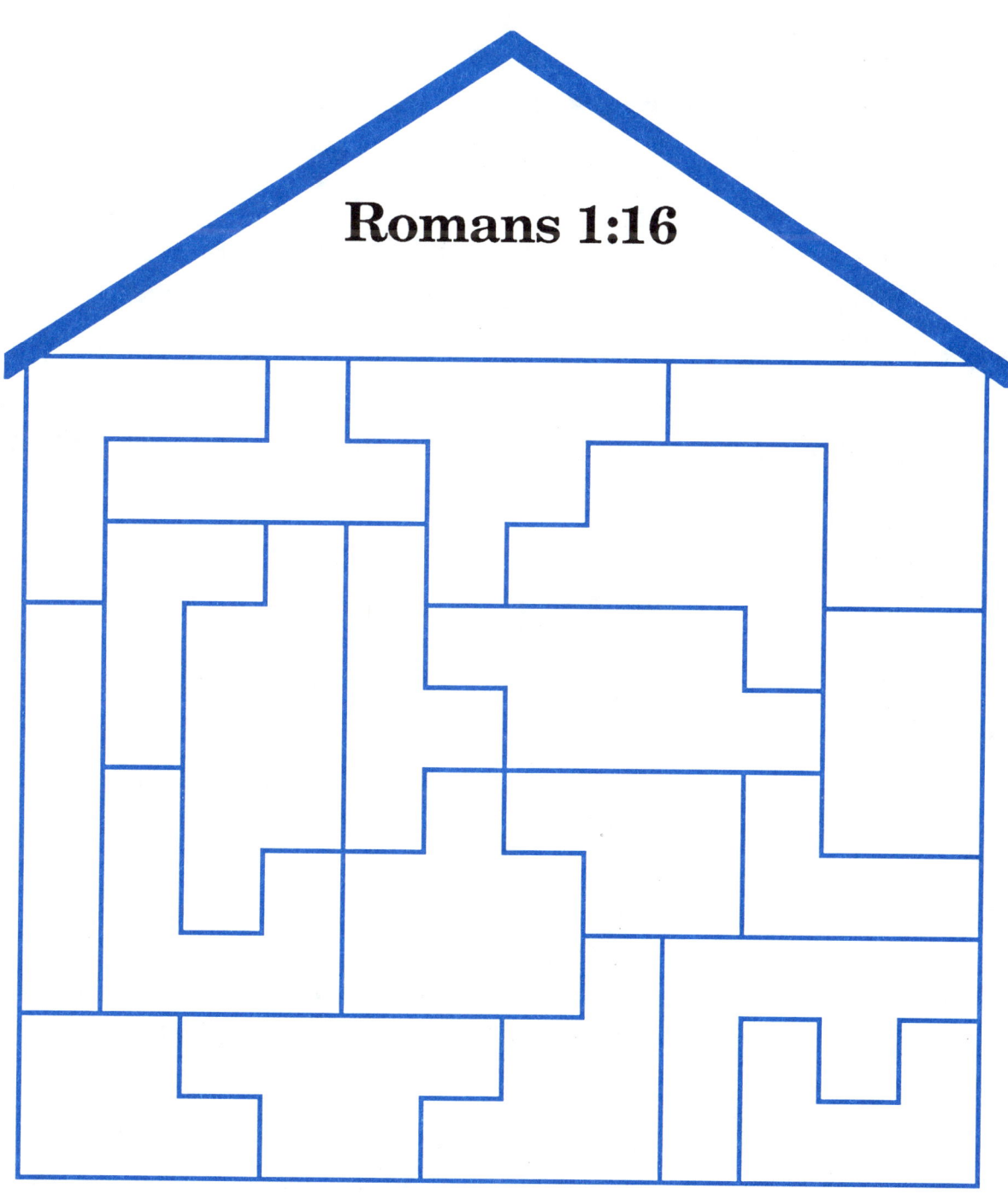

Romans 1:16

Ultimate Sacrifice

Matt. 26:57-27:33; Mark 14:53-15:21; Luke 22:54-23:26; John 18:13-19:16

I don't think any of us enjoy pain. Whether it is a cut, burn or broken arm, none of us like to get hurt. Imagine then what it must have been like for the Lord Jesus. He was beaten, slapped and spit upon. People pulled out hunks of His beard and stuck thorns into His head. They yelled and poked fun at Him, and made Him carry a heavy cross until He could not walk any further. Finally, they nailed Him to that cross where he hung for several hours and slowly suffocated to death. Still, after all this, the worse suffering Christ endured was when he took all our sins and died for them.

Since we all have sin in our hearts, we all deserve to be punished in hell. Our sin must be forgiven in order for us to have fellowship with God. In the Old Testament, the High Priest would kill a lamb and its blood was shed for the forgiveness of sin. Every year the Priest would have to do this because the blood of sheep and goats could not take away sin (Heb. 10:4).

When Jesus died, He became the ultimate sacrifice. Animals were no longer needed, because as God, Christ's death forgave all our sins. He died so that we could have eternal life. The reason the Lord Jesus suffered like this was because He was perfect and knew no sin. Christ not only died for the sins we have committed, but also for the sins we will commit in the future.

Ultimate Sacrifice

We can thank the Lord that He saw fit to forgive our sins and accept us into His heavenly family as His own beloved children.

> I am crucified with Christ: nevertheless I live; yet not I, but Christ liveth in me: and the life which I now live in the flesh I live by the faith of the Son of God, who loved me, and gave himself for me. Galatians 2:20

Color the picture which correctly matches the question.

1. What did Jesus say He could destroy and rebuild in three days?

    (Matt. 26:61)

2. In what did Jesus say they would see the Son of Man coming?

    (Matt. 26:64)

3. What did Judas cast down? (Matt. 27:5)

4. Of what was the crown made? (Matt. 27:29)

5. What did they bow before Christ while mocking Him?

(Matt. 27:29)

6. What did Peter warm himself by when he was in the high priest's

palace? (Mark 14:54)

7. With what was the temple made? (Mark 14:58)

8. What crowed? (Luke 22:60)

9. What did Simon bear? (Luke 23:26)

10. What kind of thorns did the soldiers put on Christ's head?

(John 19:2)

Ultimate Sacrifice

Find and circle the words listed in the word search puzzle. Words may be forward, backward, horizontal, vertical or diagonal.

```
G E I E K P O W E R T E S
N J E O P R I S O N E R O
A U P C D O O L B S M A T
H D D R G P I W A L P S A
E G C U I H H S N T L E R
Y M O C K E D P K B E A T
W E C I A S S I E N N C I
H N K F U Y N T H O R N S
H T E Y V G L I S O F E W
T V A R S F M E W B O L E
I V T I E K I N G D O M J
```

BEAT	JEWS	PRIEST
BLOOD	JUDGMENT	PRISONER
CAESAR	KINGDOM	PROPHESY
COCK	MOCKED	SPIT
CROWN	PILATE	TEMPLE
CRUCIFY	POWER	THORNS

Christ's Death and Resurrection

Matt. 27:31-28:15; Mark 15:20-16:11; Luke 23:26-24:12; John 19:16-20:18

Do you know what makes Christianity different from any other religion in the world? It is because Jesus rose from the dead. Other religions boast of great leaders and wonderful teachers, but these people all died, and none had the power to come back to life.

Christ's death was necessary because it provided the only way for man to get to God. In John 14:6, Jesus said, "I am the way, the truth, and the life: no man cometh unto the Father, but by me." As both God and man, Christ was the sacrifice for our sins. The reason no one can get to God except through Christ is because no one but Christ could die and raise Himself from the dead.

Christ defeated death by rising from the dead. Paul wrote in I Corinthians 15:54-55 that death is swallowed up in victory. Through belief in the Lord Jesus, we have the victory of eternal life and freedom from the curse of death.

As Christians, we do not have to fear dying because we know that Christ went there before us. Our blessed hope is that after we die we will have new bodies and a new life to spend in heaven with the Lord Jesus for eternity.

> Christ hath redeemed us from the curse of the law, being made a curse for us: for it is written, "Cursed is every one that hangeth on a tree." Galatians 3:13

Read each question and fill in the blanks from the answers in the shaded box on the next page.

1. About the _____ hour Jesus cried with a loud voice, "My God, my God, why has thou _____ me?" (Matthew 27:46)

2. When the _____ who was watching Jesus, saw the _____, and those things that were done, he _____ greatly, saying, "Truly this was the Son of God." (Matthew 27:54)

3. Joseph took Christ's body and laid it in his own new _____, and rolled a great _____ to the _____ of the sepulcher, and departed. (Matthew 27:60)

4. There was a great earthquake; for the _____ of the Lord descended from _____, and came and rolled back the stone from the door, and sat upon it. (Matthew 28:2)

5. And entering into the _____ they saw a young

man sitting on the right side, clothed in a long white _____; and they were afraid. (Mark 16:5)

6. When _____ was risen early the first day of the _____, he appeared first to _____ Magdalene. (Mark 16:9)

7. The soldiers _____ him saying, if thou be the king of the _____, save thyself. (Luke 23:37)

8. Peter ran to the tomb and saw the linen _____, laid by themselves and departed, _____ to himself at that which had come to pass. (Luke 24:12)

9. Then angels said, Woman, why _____ thou? She said, because they have _____ away my Lord, and I know not where they have _____ Him. (John 20:13)

10. Jesus said to Mary, _____ me not; for I am not yet _____ to my Father. (John 20:17)

ANGEL	GARMENT	SEPULCHER
ASCENDED	HEAVEN	STONE
CENTURION	JESUS	TAKEN
CLOTHES	JEWS	TOMB
DOOR	LAID	TOUCH
EARTHQUAKE	MARY	WEEK
FEARED	MOCKED	WEEPEST
FORSAKEN	NINTH	WONDERING

Christ's Death and Resurrection

Color in these spaces to find out the importance of Christ's resurrection. Read the remaining letters from left to right and write them on the lines in order.

Row A - 1, 2, 3, 4, 6, 8, 9	Row F - 2, 3, 4, 5, 7, 8
Row B - 1, 3, 4, 6, 7, 8, 9	Row G - 1, 5, 6, 7, 8
Row C - 2, 5, 7, 9	Row H - 1, 6, 7, 8, 9
Row D - 1, 2, 3, 5, 7, 8, 9	Row I - 1, 2, 5, 6, 7, 8, 9
Row E - 1, 2, 4, 6, 7, 9	Row J - 1, 2, 3, 4, 5, 7, 8, 9

	A	B	C	D	E	F	G	H	I	J
1	H	I	I	A	L	A	M	D	J	P
2	E	M	W	N	E	E	T	H	E	D
3	I	L	E	T	R	R	E	S	U	E
4	M	Q	R	R	N	N	E	C	T	O
5	I	O	A	T	N	E	A	A	R	U
6	S	F	N	D	O	T	T	R	O	H
7	E	H	I	B	K	R	M	S	N	T
8	E	K	L	A	I	I	Y	A	I	A
9	P	T	Y	L	R	F	E	O	F	L

___ ___ ___

___ ___ ___ ___

___ ___ ___

Christ's Ascension

Matt. 28:16-20; Luke 24:44-53; John 21:25

When we finish reading a story, there generally is a good ending which ties everything together and tells us what happens to the people. As we conclude our study on the life of the Lord Jesus, we can say with thankfulness that this story never ends.

One of the last things Christ told His followers before He ascended into heaven was that He would be with us always. Right now Christ is in heaven, preparing a place for us (John 14:2-3), and the Holy Spirit is living in our hearts, teaching and guiding our lives through the Scriptures (Ephesians 1:13-14). God is with us wherever we go; therefore, we never have to feel like we are alone.

Someday we will meet the Lord Jesus and be able to thank Him for all the wonderful things He has done. For now though, we have a job from the Lord. He told us we are to make disciples of all nations and teach them to follow the things which God has commanded (Matthew 28:19-20). It is not enough for us to believe in the Lord Jesus, we have a duty to teach other people about Him also.

> Go ye into all the world, and preach the gospel to every creature. Mark 16:15

Christ's Ascension

Read each question and write the answer from the text for this lesson.

1. Where did the eleven disciples go? (Matthew 28:16) _____

   _____

2. What did the disciples do when they saw Jesus? (Matthew 28:17)

   _____

3. Where is all power given to Jesus? (Matthew 28:18) _____

   _____

4. What are we commanded to teach? (Matthew 28:20) _____

   _____

5. What did Jesus say must be fulfilled? (Luke 24:44) _____

   _____

   _____

6. What did Jesus open? (Luke 24:45) _____

   _____

7. How long were the disciples to tarry in Jerusalem? (Luke 24:49)

   _____

8. What happened when Jesus was blessing His disciples?
   (Luke 24:51) _____

9. What were the disciples doing in the temple? (Luke 24:53) _____

   _____

10. If all the things which Jesus did were written down, how much
    space would it take? (John 21:25) _____

    _____

Write the missing words in the correct location. You will have to use your Bible and look up Matthew 28:19-20 to find the answers. These verses are the final instructions which the Lord gave us to continue His ministry on the earth. If you do not have a King James Version Bible, ask your teacher to help you with a different translation.

Go ye therefore, and teach all _____, baptizing them in the name of the _____, and of the _____, and of the _____: _____ them to observe all things whatsoever I have _____ you: And, lo, I am with you _____, even unto the end of the _____.

Christ's Ascension

As we serve the Lord, our goal is to please Him. The following verse tells us how we can do that. On the scroll below draw a picture to represent each of the missing words.

Let your ⬚ shine

before ⬚ that they

may see your good ⬚

⬚ and glorify

your Father in ⬚ .

Matthew 5:16

Cut Out Supplement

These pictures are to be cut out and pasted onto page 9.

BE KIND TO OTHERS	GO TO CHURCH	READ THE BIBLE
OBEY MY PARENTS	TELL OTHERS ABOUT JESUS	SING PRAISES TO THE LORD
LOVE MY FAMILY	PRAY FOR PEOPLE IN NEED	BRING AN OFFERING TO THE LORD
VOLUNTEER TO HELP CLEAN MY CHURCH	VISIT SOMEONE IN THE HOSPITAL	

Fill in your own gift

Cut Out Supplement

These pictures are to be cut out and pasted onto page 37.

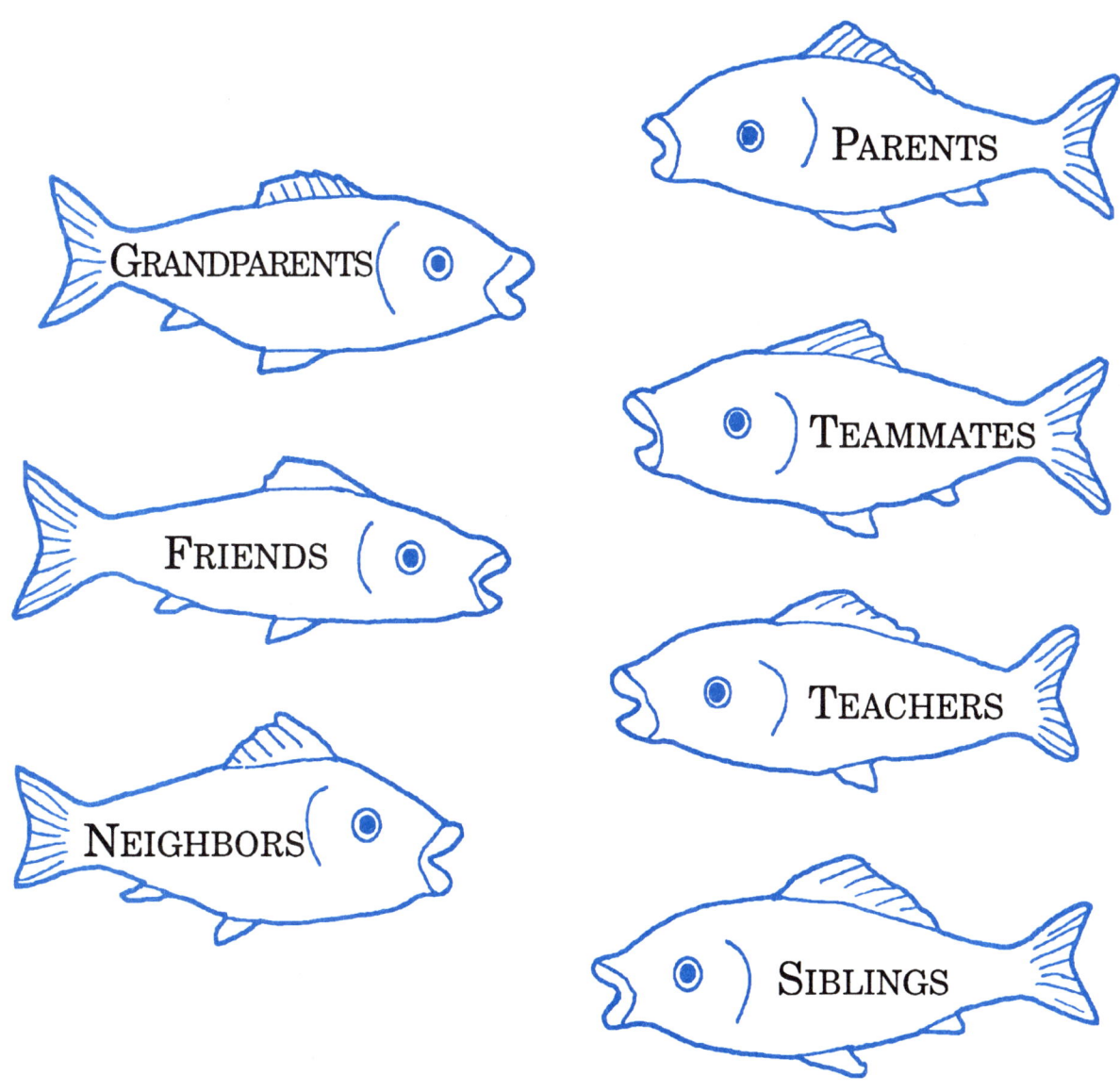

Cut Out Supplement

These pictures are to be cut out for the project on pages 44 and 45.

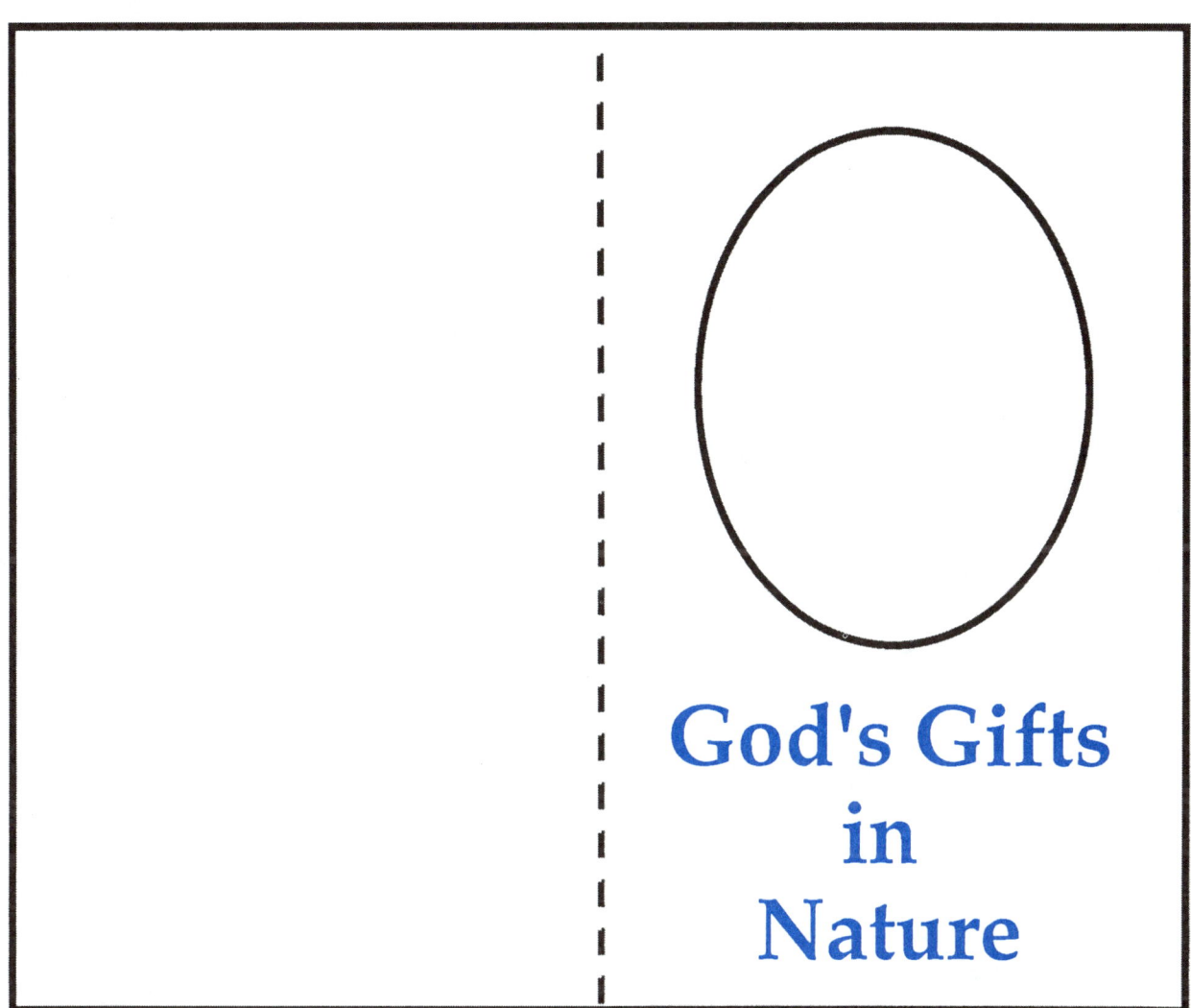

**God's Gifts
in
Nature**

*The Heavens
are thine.*

Ps. 89:11

Cut Out Supplement

These pictures are to be cut out for the project on pages 44 and 45.

I form the Light

Isa. 45:7

The mountains shall bring peace to the people

Ps. 72:3

He leadeth me beside the still waters.

Ps. 23:2

For the tree is known by his fruit.

Matt. 12:33

Cut Out Supplement

These pictures are to be cut out for the project on pages 44 and 45.

**The earth is full
of the goodness
of the Lord**

Ps. 33:5

**And I will
send grass**

Deut. 11:15

Cut Out Supplement

These pictures are to be cut out and pasted onto page 56.

Cut Out Supplement

These pictures are to be cut out for the project on pages 104 and 105.

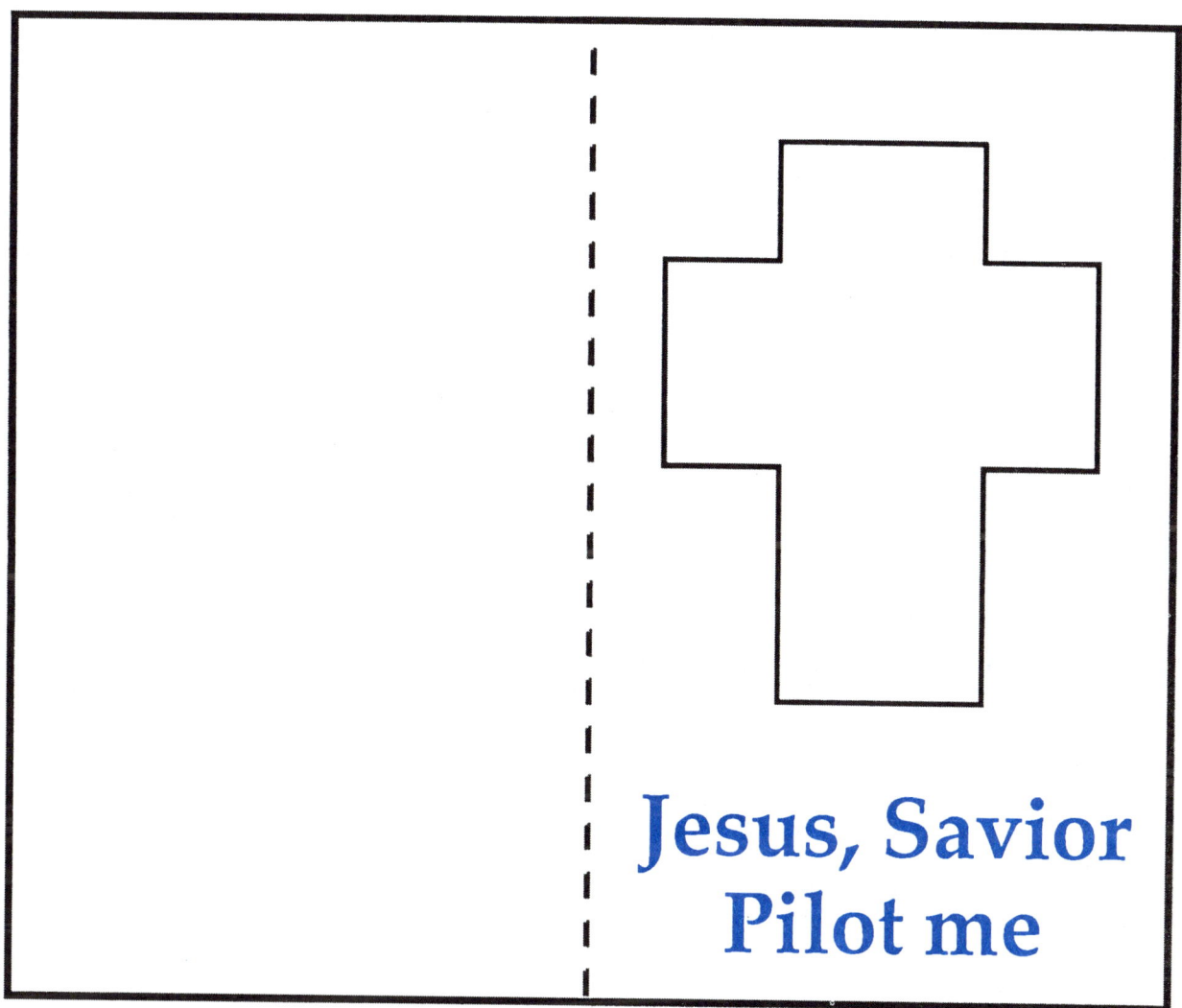

Jesus, Savior Pilot me

Jesus, Savior pilot me

Cut Out Supplement

These pictures are to be cut out for the project on pages 104 and 105.

Wondrous Sov'reign of the sea

Chart and compass came from thee

Over life's tempestuous sea

Jesus, Savior pilot me

Cut Out Supplement

These puzzle pieces are to be cut out and pasted onto page 109.

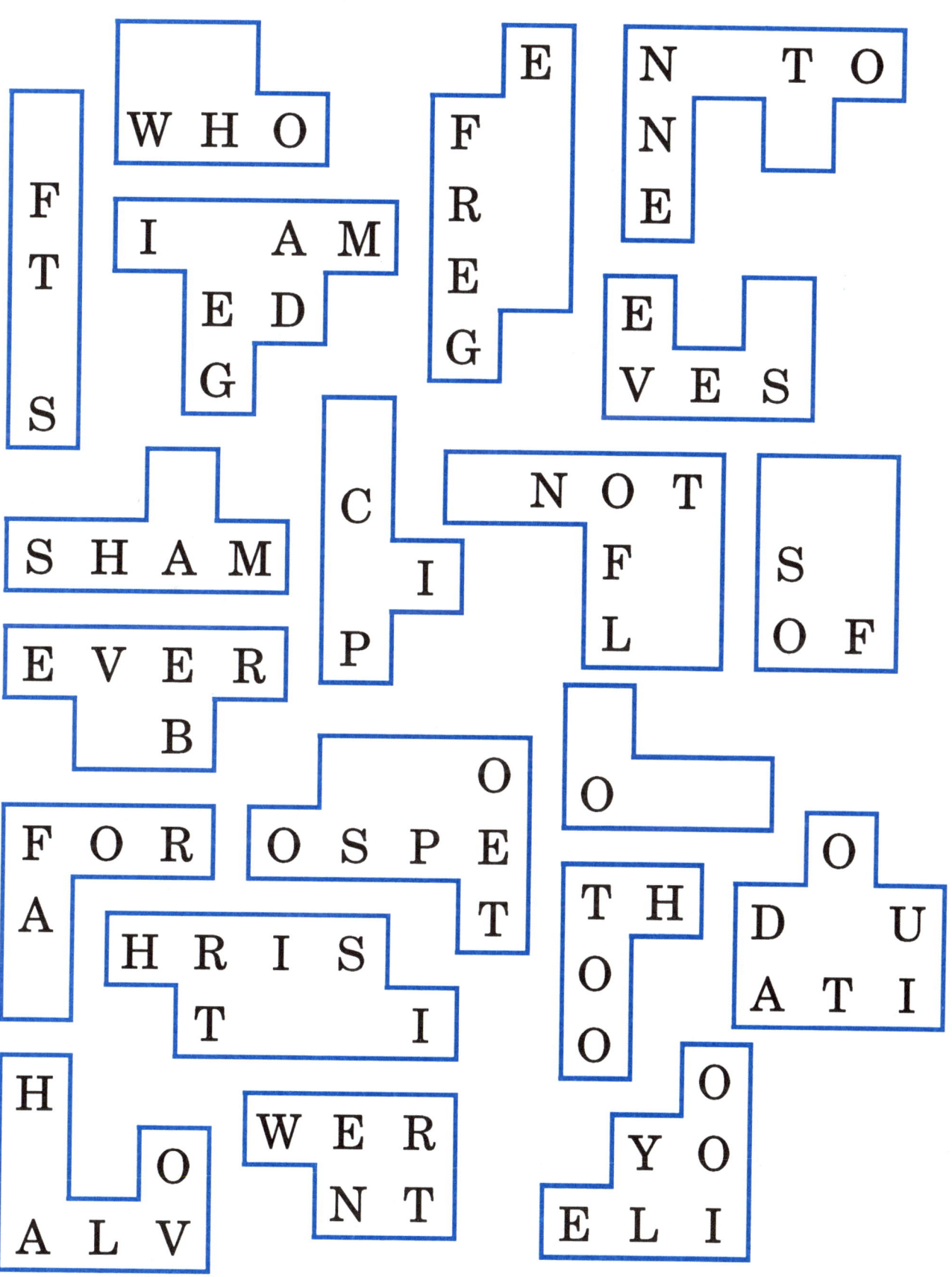